Dear Divine,
Thank you for the gift of eloquence.
Help me to know what to say in this world of words.

***

Thank you to our dearly departed Sean Armstrong.
He knew I would write this book before I did.

Thank you friends and family
for living this great experiment with me.

Thank *you* for seeking.
Seek and you shall find.

***

"The lips of wisdom are closed,
except to the ears of Understanding." [1]

***

The subject tonight is Love.
And for tomorrow night as well.
As a matter of fact, I know of no better
topic for us to discuss until we all die!
– Hafiz: 14th Century Sufi Poet [2]

As Within, So Without:
Love Yourself, Love the World

KAREN NEVERLAND

Copyright © Neverland Publications 2012
Cover design by Karen Neverland

All rights reserved.

ISBN-13: 978-0615721545
ISBN-10: 0615721540

CONTENTS

Introduction   7

1. Love   13

2. Ego   33

3. Fear   47

4. Suffering   57

5. Desire   71

6. Ignorance   85

7. Compassion   101

8. Anger   119

9. Consciousness   131

10. Balance   145

11. Aloneness   157

12. Honesty   167

13. Purpose   183

Inconclusive Conclusion…   193

Journey On: Influences and Other Sources   197

References   199

About Karen Neverland: When the Skies Turn Red   213

INTRODUCTION

> I have shown you the path to liberation;
> know that liberation depends on you.
> – Siddhartha Gautama: Founder of Buddhism [1]

I used to go to the library looking for a book of answers. I would skim the shelves and look for the answer to all of my questions. I did not know what my questions were exactly, but I knew there were questions. I knew there was something I was not getting, something I was not answering, something that everyone else *must* know because I seemed to be the only one who searched. I felt lost and alone.

Most of my life has been a quest to find those answers. Through endless journeying I found that answers cannot be given in a book or told to us by someone else. If there was a solution that worked for everyone, we would each be born with a book on how to win this "Game of Life." Clearly this is not the case.

Truth cannot be milled down into easily digestible sound-bites because it comes in the form of *experience*. Wisdom is revealed to us as we walk this Great Path and it is a way of thinking and living.

The Wisdom we attain from life is too profound to pass on through language. As we travel, the complexities of the Universe reveal themselves to us and we understand them from a place deep within ourselves. No one can explain these to us.

I wrote this book as an aid to you in your quest. I have not written this book so that you will copy my every action. I illustrate my path with this transparency to illuminate other options than the ones given to us. I hand you a torch, but I cannot light it for you. You will find the light, and you will walk this path alone.

> A disciple…can never imitate his guide's steps. You have your own way of living your life, of dealing with problems, and of winning. Teaching is only demonstrating that it is possible. Learning is making it possible for yourself.
> – Paulo Coelho: Poet and Writer [2]

This is not meant to be a play-by-play; it is a guidebook. I have studied endlessly in a quest to piece ideas together and form a worldview that makes sense. I have carefully crafted theories only to later have them crumble completely. Through this trial and error, I have found a path that sees the world as Divine. I invite you to join me in this Beautiful World; whether it is this way or your own way.

This book explains the pattern that I have used to describe existence and it works for me. Living in this fashion has led to a profound level of true happiness. I share it in the hope that it does the same for you. What you get out of this book depends on you and what you are willing to let go, experience, and accept about yourself. No one can force you to grow; that is your choice.

This work is meant to get you thinking and asking questions. In *The Matrix,* Trinity says, "It's the question that drives us… It's the question that brought you here. You know the question, just as I did… The answer is out there…and it's looking for you, and it will find you if you want it to." [3] I hope to help you formulate some of your own questions so you can figure out your own answers. After all, we cannot find The Answer until we know what questions to ask. Let your questions drive you forward and learn to use discernment when you process information; these are the keys to true Wisdom.

If it brings happiness, keep it. As soon as it no longer brings happiness, discard it. Do not attach to anything. Make mistakes, but keep learning. Winston Churchill said, "You will make all kinds of mistakes; but as long as you are generous and true and also fierce you cannot hurt the world or even seriously distress her." [4]

Do not feel hopeless as you wander. We often mistake the destination as the purpose for the journey, but it might just be that The Meaning of Life is to find and create a meaning for life. Keep walking forward and you can reach any destination.

> Not all those who wander are lost.
> – J.R.R. Tolkien: Writer and Professor [5]

This book can assist you in finding your true-self, but know that you cannot become "better" than you *are*. You *are You*. You cannot change who you *are*, but you can change the method you go through life and the level of happiness you experience on the way. We choose the path of suffering to teach ourselves the lessons we want to learn, but this is not the only path; love and acceptance can teach us the same lessons that suffering can. When we discover our true-selves and our true heart's desires, we are able to act, grow, and live in ways that bring immense joy for all.

As the human race evolves and multiplies, it is important that we look at ourselves and analyze the suffering that comes from within. Carl Jung said, "When we reach a higher cultural level, we must forgo compulsion and turn to self-development." [6] That time is Now. The more of us there are on the planet, the more important it becomes to be responsible for our actions. A world of nearly seven-billion people cannot support our animalistic and instinctual mistakes for long. We can and must evolve in order to continue our survival, and more importantly, to promote our collective happiness.

As much as we try to deny it, the planet Earth is one gigantic life form, like a body made up of trillions of cells. If we live only for ourselves, we become a destructive cancer cell that divides endlessly for its own gain at the expense of the cells around it. When we live in harmony, we live as one healthy planet. It seems easier to blame others for our own misconduct than to take responsibility for ourselves, but this method of living is no longer serving us. Accountability for our actions, and allowing ourselves to understand how they affect life as a whole, frees us to move forward and create change.

We cannot change the world by forcing others to change; we can only look at ourselves. As we change within, the world outside of us also changes. Our internal worldview influences the world around us. Kahlil Gibran said, "Even as the holy and righteous cannot rise beyond the highest which is in each of you, so the wicked and the weak cannot fall lower than the lowest which is in you also." [7] When we learn to look within, we find that all of the collective insanity of the planet is within us also.

We have put off our personal development in favor of instant gratification and pleasure distractions. Now is the time to look within ourselves and evolve. Carl Jung also said, "People will do anything, no matter how absurd, in order to avoid facing their own soul." [8] In some ways, it is easier to run away, but I ask you to step outside of your comfort zone and step within yourself. You will find the darkest darks and the lightest lights, but it is worth it. As you work through your deepest darkest secrets, the world changes before your very eyes and reforms into a spectacular paradise.

At times personal progress seems slow and difficult; it feels like we work very hard and accomplish very little. Remember that even the smallest change in thought and deed has an infinite effect on the Universe. Lao Tzu said, "The journey of a thousand miles starts from beneath your feet." [9] When you get discouraged, look where you are and realize how far you have come.

> Even a tiny drop of a powerful tincture can
> change the color of the entire glass of water.
> – Alex Grey: Visionary Artist [10]

I wrote this book with the idea that we all belong to One Religion: the Religion of Love. Love is universal. The 13th century poet Rumi said, "I go into the Muslim mosque and the Jewish synagogue and the Christian church and I see one altar." [11] Another Sufi poet, Hafiz, said, "The temple, the synagogue, the church, and the mosque are all houses of love." [12] Diversity of religious teachings is beautiful, but we let our differences divide us rather than let our similarities unite us. I hope you will let Love unify us all together. We are all on this Quest of Life, no matter where it takes us and what methods we apply. We share this world with every life-form on it.

Through this book, I hope to share love, understanding, a connection, and a vibration on whatever planes you believe in. Perhaps this written experiment will help you awaken into yourself. There are many concepts that I do not understand about you and the world, and the words that are true Today may not be true tomorrow, but the Love will always come across. Love is a Force deep within us that transcends all experiences here on Earth. That Force will change you, if you let it.

Now, delve into that space. I will meet you there.

1. LOVE

> Love fills everything. It cannot be desired because it is an end in itself. It cannot betray because it has nothing to do with possession. It cannot be held prisoner because it is a river and will overflow its banks. Anyone who tries to imprison love will cut off the spring that feeds it, and the trapped water will grow stagnant and rank.
> – Paulo Coelho: Poet and Writer [1]

Love is magic. Music, movies, books, and poetry are dedicated solely to the explanation of this overwhelming Force. Yet, even with all our attempts, we do not truly understand the essence of it. We are wrapped up in the expedition of love, but our excavations rarely reveal the true gems that we struggle and strive for. Many of us never find the full-blown ineffable power of Love, though we search our entire lives for it.

The early stages of infatuation get mistaken for Love and we find ourselves day-dreaming of a perfectly impossible person who will "fix" our lives for us. We are twitter pated with passion, sex, extravagance, and excitement, while seeking constant pleasure and the promise of newness. This quest unleashes a world of expectations upon our relationships and many of them do not last long past this initial flirtation. Dating and acquiring partners shakes up our world and makes us believe that life is changing into the paradise we envision. When these games inevitably end, we believe that the love is over and the passion has died. We think that the "spark" left and we abandon our "feelings."

The closer we get to someone, the more corrosions and imperfections we discover. These revelations lead to feelings of betrayal and anger because we believed the false image they showed to us, so when the truth is revealed, we feel lied to. We run away at the sight of the damaged and broken person beneath. We lie to ourselves and say that we just "fell out of love," but we did not love them in the first place; we just enjoyed having a distraction from our own lives for a while. It sounds harsh, but we often use people to satisfy our own needs rather than loving them. When accepting someone gets difficult, we believe that the spark is just "gone." This is when our so-called "love" dies.

When the blinding passion has leveled off, love is just beginning. When the show is over and we meet the real person backstage, we start to see the aspects that we previously ignored and we are offered the opportunity to really love them. Relationships get scary at this point because we begin to understand each other and see the darker pieces that were previously overlooked. Love becomes difficult when the shiny, new polish has worn off and we want the fresh relationship back again.

We think of attachment to other people as love, because it feels satisfying to be with them and it feels empty to be without them, but this is a selfish-based emotion and it is a far cry away from True Love. Showy examples of love are the attempts of our minds to pursue and conquer someone else. Flirtation forms a temporary spell that consumes our sanity and replaces it with obsession. We use people to fulfill our needs and then we become dependant on them to fulfill those needs.

The instant gratification of relationships is a distraction that is easy to latch on to. It is easier to believe that someone loves us if they serve us. There is a feeling of fulfillment and contentment that comes with indulgence and we mistake this satisfaction with love. When we are taken care of and provided for, we feel nurtured and safe. This type of "love" is all about us and what another person can do for us. Real Love is more than money and date nights.

We believe that love is given to us by others, that it will come into our lives via a special person, and that there is one individual who will turn our lives upside down and change them for the better. This belief causes us to search externally for something that others cannot give us.

We cannot be given Love. People can act loving toward us, but in the end, we choose how to feel. If people gave us emotions, the moment someone loved us, we would love them in return because they would give us the feeling. If Jake is in love with Sally, then Sally *must* be in love with Jake, because he gives her the feeling of love. This is not the case because we choose how to feel. As long as we search externally for Love through fulfillment of desires, we never find it.

Unconditional Acceptance

> Our job is to love others without stopping to inquire whether or not they are worthy. That is not our business and, in fact, it is nobody's business. What we are asked to do is to love; and this love itself will render both ourselves and our neighbor worthy if anything can.
> – Thomas Merton: Writer and Mystic [2]

Unconditional acceptance is the root of True Love. It is difficult to love someone's imperfections, but it is only when we accept and love *all* parts of a person that we love *them*. If we only love *part* of someone, picking and choosing pieces to love, we do not love *them*. Ignoring certain aspects of a person and creating others forms people into imaginary concepts; then we love those ideas, not the people themselves. We "fall in love" with their façade and secretly hate their true-self. This idea of "love" is selfish and self-serving; it creates others into a specific idea that we have for them and we do not take the time to learn who they really *are*.

Unconditional acceptance is a state of acknowledging a person, situation, or thing for what it is, without judgment or restriction, and embracing it. Unconditional acceptance means that we allow life to exist as it *is*, whether we agree with it or not, and do not attempt to change or alter it. This can be difficult, but it is essential to creating loving relationships. Understanding and accepting all parts of a person reveals the true, overwhelming power of Love and frees us to build relationships on a foundation of understanding of who people *are*, rather than who we expect them to be. Writer Neale Donald Walsch said:

> To be totally loving means to be willing to give every mature sentient being total freedom to be, do, and have that which they wish. … Let go of expectation, let go of requirements and rules and regulations that you would impose on your loved ones. For they are not loved if they are restricted. … Indeed, if you believe their choices to have been poor ones, that is precisely the time to show your love.[3]

The love that comes from unconditional acceptance is much more challenging than flirtation and indulgence, so we run away, not realizing that True Love is what we actually seek. The Bible says in 1 Corinthians 13:4–8:

> Love is patient, love is kind. It does not envy, it does not boast, it is not proud. It does not rude, it is not self-seeking, it is not easily angered, it keeps no record of wrongs. Love does not delight in evil but rejoices with the truth. It always protects, always trusts, always hopes, always perseveres. Love never fails.[4]

This definition of Love far surpasses the shallow emptiness that we often experience.

Many of our relationships are founded on non-acceptance and need. We make demands and expectations on people and we only "love" them if they continue to fulfill those expectations. The moment our needs stop being fulfilled, we believe that we are no longer in love. We say statements like: "I love her *when* she smiles," "I love him *if* he is there for me," or "I love them *because* they are funny." This is conditional love. It requires a qualification to be met in order for us to keep feeling the way we do. "I love you *if*…" We only show affection when the stipulations that we set are satisfied.

When we pursue people out of conditional love, we give away the power to make decisions in our own lives. We create a condition, and when people do what we want, we "love" them; when they do not, we do not love them. Either way, our feelings rely exclusively on the actions of someone else to maintain them. "I love you *if*…" and it is then up to them to satisfy that "if."

Once we put ourselves in this state, we need others to fulfill love for us, because we are incapable of satisfying our own needs and we need someone else to do it for us. We shut off our own springs of Love and seek it externally.

Others can never give us enough love to satisfy our needs, so we attempt to force our agenda and control others until we acquire the desired feelings and actions. This is a common misconception about love. We believe that we must shape ourselves and our relationships into a situation that "works" and that by changing ourselves and our fellow beings, we can hammer our relationships into "better" ones.

Many of our relationships are formed with this combination of repression and ignorance. We long for Love, so we conform to our lover's wishes. We hide parts of ourselves and ignore parts of others. In turn, we make demands on others to take part in the self-repression. We need our relationships, so we do whatever possible to maintain them. In the process, we suppress each other and ourselves until our relationships are reduced to the fake and empty interactions of conceptual people that do not really exist. Then we wonder why we feel so lost.

When we navigate relationships with expectations and demands, we restrict who it is acceptable for people to be and they cannot be themselves. We "love" the conceptual idea of who a person is, but refuse to see and understand the real person below. If we press our agenda upon others until they conform and then they later stop conforming, (and they will,) the relationship dies.

Conditional love is a self-serving lie. People are not what they own, do, or say; these are external additions on themselves and they can be subtracted or changed at any time; loving these additions is a fallacy.

Unconditional Love does not try to change people, even if we personally disagree with their choices. Love does not need certain decisions for its own benefit. Real Love wants to be with people, rather than needs them; it does not ignore flaws, it thrives on them.

This state of Love does not require that we are perfect, only that we accept imperfections unconditionally.

Love is a constant and never withdraws itself. It is impossible to "fall out of love," because it is within and requires no external conditions to continue. Without conditions, Love cannot stop because nothing can "happen" to bring about that end; we keep accepting others, regardless of fights, breakups, betrayal, lies, etc. Even if our relationship with a person concludes and we part ways, Love remains, because external occurrences cannot change it. This is the true state of Love that is within us. Once the conditions are removed, we open ourselves up to feel the Love that naturally bubbles up inside of us. Once our "qualifications" are gone, we discover Love as it *exists* within each and every one of us, at every moment. The eyes of an infant watch and accept all that happens, without judgment; this is our natural state.

Acceptance is the difference between conditional and unconditional love. When we accept ourselves and others, it encourages us to grow and be whoever we naturally *are*. This understanding and acceptance forms a bond of respect between life-forms that cannot be broken, and this is what True Love *is*. Acceptance is a personal choice that allows us to *live in Love*.

When we do not experience Love within ourselves, we require an external source for it. We can imagine ourselves as empty cups: When we fill ourselves with the waters of Love, we overflow and it emanates from us in tidal waves. If we instead attempt to give love away, then we are always in a lack and seeking to be filled.

If we do not feel Love within, we have to find it without. In this state, we feel that there is not enough to go around and we hesitate to be the first to say, "I love you," in case the other person does not feel the same way. We always feel empty and we need others to "fix" it. Love like this requires a constant state of renewal in order to stay alive: dates, presents, kissing, sex, cuddling, etc. We fear to give love away because we do not know if we will get it back.

True Love does not require a return on its investment because "giving" someone love does not diminish our supply at all. Real Love is a candle that can light many other candles without ever diminishing itself. When we generate the unconditional feeling of acceptance from within, there is no way to diminish it. We can feel it for every person that we meet. The more we love, the more Love we experience. It is that simple.

Self-Love

> We know that we do not conquer thirst by repressing it.
> – C.G. Jung: Founder of Analytical Psychology [5]

From a very young age, we learn that certain aspects of us are acceptable, while others are not. Each time we act "unacceptable," we learn to hold that quality within us and pretend it does not exist. The mind then hides our repressions from us through a series of self-hate games and repeatedly tells us that certain aspects of ourselves are not acceptable. On the other hand, each time we act and get rewarded, we amplify and distort that aspect. Both of these processes create a false-self that disguises the true-self and traps it within.

The more we disapprove and hate ourselves, the more we repress. The more we repress, the more we disapprove and hate. This abuse makes us feel empty, because we are trapped inside and completely unfulfilled. In this lethargic state, we feel so barren and depleted that we need someone else to come along and "complete" us. We feel like something is missing until someone comes and "fills up our holes."

These ideas about love reflect our inner-selves and what is going on inside of us. Our external world is a reflection of our internal world. We miss ourselves, so we seek others to complete us. We interpret and project the world on the outside that we believe in on the inside and we form relationships with people based on the ideas we hold on to. If we have fake, empty love for others, it is because of the fake, empty love we have for ourselves. When we do not experience Unconditional Love within, we do not experience it without.

It seems brutal to admit that we hate ourselves, but that is what happens when we do not accept unconditionally. When we only accept parts of ourselves, we do not accept at all. We form conditional love, thinking: "I love you *if* you keep these certain aspects hidden."

Hate is conditional acceptance: we despise, disapprove, and seek to change something as it *exists*. When we love part of ourselves and exaggerate other parts, we form ourselves into an illusionary "concept of self," rather than discover our true-selves.

Self-hate causes hatred, fear, and suffering in the world. Repression of the self causes immense internal pain, which we then target onto people around us. When we cause internal suffering for ourselves, we make up external "reasons" for our internal pain. It seems easier to target external sources for our suffering than delve within and discover what lies there.

We cannot be our true-selves if we repress ourselves. As we repress, we form a dichotomy between the true-self and the projected-self. Aspects of our true-selves are stored deep inside of us and we become less and less capable of connecting with others on a real level. The more we repress ourselves, the more self-hate there is holding the true-self in the subconscious. This causes us to stop living in a state of unconditional acceptance and shut off the springs of Love.

No matter how strongly we deceive and repress ourselves, eventually our repressions claw their way to the surface. Carl Jung explained that the unconscious becomes quite dangerous when our conscious mind does not accept it:

> [The unconscious] is dangerous only when our conscious attitude toward it becomes hopelessly false. And this danger grows in the measure that we practice repressions. But as soon as the patient begins to assimilate the contents that were previously unconscious, the danger from the side of the unconscious diminishes. As the process of assimilation goes on, it puts an end to the dissociation of the personality and to the anxiety that attends and inspires the two realms of the psyche. [6]

Repression creates inner demons. We can mask these subconscious-monsters as long as we keep people at a distance, but the closer we get to each other, the harder it gets to hide them. When the behemoth parts of us, our friends, and our families rear their ugly heads, it is easy to cast blame and be upset. We do not realize that we may have assisted in the repression-demon by refusing to accept a person in the first place.

The unaccepted parts of ourselves form our repressed self or shadow. When we want to be better or we imagine ourselves as better, the shadow-self is created and hidden from our consciousness. The more we strive to hide this shadow, the darker it becomes. [7] The less we accept our true-selves and the true-selves of others, the stronger our shadows become.

Unconditional acceptance dissolves internal demons, because they are able to come to the surface. When we flood our shadows with light, they disappear. As we unconditionally accept ourselves and others, it heals all wounds, no matter how deep they are.

Real Love understands that subconscious-monsters exist and is not surprised when seemingly-horrific attributes arise. In the state of Love, we accept even the darkest side of people and welcome those flaws with smiles and embraces, knowing it is more helpful to have them out than in. It is a great honor when someone shares their inner-demons with us; it means that we are trusted enough for them to do so. If we react with anger or repression toward someone who shares these, their dichotomy of self gets stronger. If we act in acceptance and understanding, that demon dissipates. We do not have to stay with people who hurt us, but we want to accept them unconditionally and move on.

It is nearly impossible to accept and love others when we are distracted fighting an inner battle. We cannot put our true-selves on display if we dislike parts of that self. Likewise, we cannot love others if there is hate festering inside of us. Hiding parts of ourselves leads to secrecy and lies in every interaction we have. Starting our relationships out with deception causes them to fall apart.

We cannot love anyone else until we love ourselves, because we feel Love within and it extends outward. Yet, many of us do not love ourselves because of an extreme amount of repression and self-hate.

Healing self-hate is difficult, because our minds hide it from us. Most of us do not know that we hate ourselves. If we realized our internal battle against ourselves, we would be forced to resolve it, so our minds keep it hidden.

In the mind's genius scheme to hide our self-hate, it uses self-inflation to cover it up. We repress ourselves with self-hate; then we repress the self-hate with self-inflation.[8] This leads to a double-blind mask that maintains the repression of the true-self.

In order to discover the state of Love, we have to get past the idea that "I am the greatest person ever, of course I love myself." We cannot start hearing the self-hate and working with it until we admit that we lie to ourselves about our internal state. Before we can learn to love ourselves, we must admit the possibility that we do not love ourselves. Some of us cannot even admit this one fact. We call our self-hate, "constructive criticism" or "self improvement," when we really mean: "I will be better someday," and "I am not good enough."

We experience self-hate *every time* we refuse to accept ourselves. This can be a small quick act of criticism or an all out war against the self. You have experienced a moment of self-hate if you have ever:

1. Criticized, judged, or disliked aspects of yourself or others.
2. Struggled with being alone, loneliness, or silence.
3. Treated yourself or your body poorly: unhealthy eating habits, lack of exercise, sleep deprivation, laziness.
4. Spent time or wasted time doing things you do not like doing.
5. Avoided creating and meeting achievable goals.
6. Been addicted to a substance, person, or behavioral pattern.
7. Been unable to accept a situation or person as they *exist*, Right Now.
8. Doubted yourself or been unsure of what to do.

All of these are done in a moment of non-acceptance or self-hate. Perhaps we do not hate ourselves all the time, but when we refuse to accept ourselves *for even a moment*, we experience repression and hatred. Like the 2010 movie *Inception*, when we place ideas in the deepest recesses of our minds, they grow exponentially by the time they reach our conscious mind. Likewise, even small acts of repression can define us and our actions. This is why it is important to heal *all* self-hate. The smallest moment of non-acceptance can lead to large issues that then define and restrict us.

Forgiveness

> To err is human, to forgive is divine.
> – Alexander Pope: 18th Century Poet [9]

Forgiveness is the key to Unconditional Love. Forgiveness is the total acceptance of flaws and loving regardless. When we accept, it means we forgive ourselves and others for all faults, knowing that our flaws make us perfect.

Unconditional Love is experienced when we respect and accept, regardless of behavior or appearance. In this sort of Love, we desire everyone to be free and to be themselves, because we accept everyone for who they *are*; we know that we could not make anyone better, even if they make mistakes, because their mistakes are a part of their exploration of life. The person who makes mistakes and learns is the one that we love.

> Forgiveness is part of the treasure you need
> to craft your falcon wings and return to
> your true realm of Divine freedom.
> – Hafiz: 14th Century Sufi Poet [10]

Forgiveness is not just about others, it is about us. When we forgive, we release the harmful feelings from within ourselves and choose not to dwell on them. Instead of focusing on harmful aspects of a person, we let them go and choose to understand them as a perfectly flawed individual. This frees both parties from the attachment to suffering.

Forgiveness starts with forgiveness of the self. If we harbor anger and resentment toward ourselves, we then seek to push these feelings upon the world. As we learn to be compassionate and forgiving toward ourselves, it becomes easier to reflect this onto the outside world. There is nothing "wrong" with anyone. It all just *is*. We can accept it or not, but our opinions will not change what happened, is happening, or will happen.

Shifting Within

> The capacity to love others depends
> on the capacity to love ourselves.
> – Thich Nhat Hanh: Buddhist Monk and Writer [11]

We are our own worst enemies, but we know ourselves more than anyone else. When we learn to love and accept ourselves in every way possible, it is easy to accept those around us. Once we visit the strongest of demons in ourselves, we can understand the demons of others. We all have the same demons, they just have different faces.

Self-acceptance does not mean we get to pick and choose which qualities of ours to accept. It means that we learn to accept *all of them* as they *exist,* Right Now. When we love ourselves, our lives are free to change and grow as we do.

There are thousands of ways we attack ourselves on a daily basis, (weight, intelligence, job, money, relationships, family, talents, etc.) but we hide this abuse in our minds and project a different person on the outside. The catch is, no matter how well we hide this abuse, we secretly know about it and that makes us feel inadequate.

The more we repress feelings, the more vicious they become inside of us. The more we project a false-person on the outside, the more we hate ourselves for the lies. Hiding false projections from ourselves requires a great deal of energy and we find ourselves acting in ways we do not like, surrounding ourselves with people who hurt us, and living in a state of total unhappiness. These are the attempts of the subconscious to hide our repressions.

The less true we are with ourselves, the less true we can be with other people. The more we project a false-person, the more we distrust others' images. It goes on and on until we are so distrusting and fake that we feel isolated and alone. We then play games to acquire other people's love, since we are unable to feel it within ourselves. Instead, we can learn to stop fighting against ourselves and let ourselves *be*.

> Whenever you are confronted with an opponent conquer him with love.
> – Mahatma Gandhi: Activist [12]

Real Love is a state of non-expectation. In this state, all that occurs, no matter how difficult, is perfect for us at that moment. We accept life unconditionally and love it for what it *is*. This uninhibited state of Love is the pervasive Force that penetrates every aspect of existence and reveals joy, passion, and the thirst for life. Unconditional Love puts our emotions into our own hands; it empowers us. It is now our decision to decide how we feel and interact in this life, and that perspective decides *everything*.

We expend extreme amounts of energy to avoid delving into our inner-selves, but love and acceptance is a happier way to live. Ben Stewart said in his documentary, *Kymatica* (2009):

> We can deal with wars, we can deal with terrorism, we can deal with stock market collapse and economic collapse. We can deal with these things, but once we start to notice this chaos within ourselves that's what we're really afraid of. We'll take a million September 11ths over one moment of true insight toward our self-hate.[13]

Outer battles have nothing on inner battles. We play mind-games to escape the understanding and acceptance of ourselves. When we live in forgiveness, acceptance, and compassion, we learn to cultivate unconditional acceptance for the person we hate the most in the whole world: ourselves. We can then reflect our internal state upon the external world.

The world acts as a mirror for us. The qualities we dislike about others are projections of ourselves onto them. We have a direct picture of ourselves through our experience of our fellow man. We act cruel toward others through the redirection of our self-loathing. Our external acts of hatred and destructiveness begin with internal self-hate and self-destructiveness. [14]

We cannot change the world by forcing other people to change. We can only live by example. Gandhi said, "I…realize more and more the infinite possibilities of universal love," [15] and also, "We need to be the change we wish to see in the world." [16] There are infinite possibilities with Love, and we can create a happier world by starting with ourselves. It is infinitely easier to "Love your neighbor as yourself," [17] when we actually love ourselves.

> The more you are motivated by love, the more
> fearless and free your action will be.
> – Unknown [18]

Love allows an acceptance of how life *is*, which results in freedom and fearlessness. You deserve to have this Love in your life. Every creature deserves Love. It is our birthright. Siddhartha Gautama said, "Searching in all directions with one's awareness, one finds no one dearer than oneself. In the same way, others are fiercely dear to themselves. So one should not hurt others if one loves oneself." [19]

Do not believe for a second that you (or anyone else) do not deserve to be loved. We are wonderful creations. When we restrict ourselves, we place ourselves into a mould that we cannot quite fit into. When we unbind ourselves, we can see the Divine Person that each of us *is*.

Practice!

At the end of each chapter there are ways to practice the concepts discussed. You do not have to do them. I have done all of these and they helped me immensely. I recommend giving them a try. If they do not work for you, then stop, or use them to form your own exercises. The main goal is for you to start actively working with yourself, freeing yourself, and letting yourself grow.

1. Get to know yourself. Find a mirror somewhere private and spend at least five minutes consciously talking to yourself. Look yourself in the eyes and talk until you feel like stopping. You cannot develop a relationship with someone you never talk to, and you no doubt have a lot of catching up to do!
2. Stop all self-criticism. It is *not* constructive. View your mind as a lost puppy and help it to find its way home. Always respond to yourself in Love. You are the moon, and your "flaws" are a cloud covering you up. Even at the darkest moments, you still shine the same.
3. Whenever you notice a destructive thought:
   1. Acknowledge the thought and why you feel that way.
   2. Tell yourself that you do not agree with the thought and replace it with a helpful one.
   3. Remind yourself that you love and accept yourself, even though you have critical thoughts.
4. Make a list of affirmations: loving statements about yourself. Speak these affirmations daily.
5. Start a meditation practice. This is your moment to sit and be with yourself. Enjoy this time to bask in the awesome person that you *are*. Find yourself. Above all, be patient.
6. **Questions: Find your own questions. Find your own answers. These may help you get started:**
   What is Love?
   Is there a difference between self-love and vanity/pride?
   What is criticism and why does it exist?

2. EGO

> Each of us is something of a schizophrenic
> personality, tragically divided against ourselves.
> – Martin Luther King, Jr.: Nobel Peace Prize [1]

The ego is a complicated creature that is difficult to define. Psychology explains that the ego serves as the conscious mediator between a person and their reality. [2] Buddhism says that the ego and "self" are illusions of the skandhas. [3] Hinduism teaches that the ahamkara (ego) is on the outside of the inner Self; the inner Self is always at peace. [4] More recently, Eckhart Tolle discussed that the ego is a self-centered, compulsory voice within our heads that hijacks our minds and is always struggling to protect and enlarge itself. [5]

All of these views share a common idea: The ego is not us. We each have an ego that voices our "thoughts" and a true-self that is aware of those thoughts. Any voice that chatters in our heads is the ego; it is the "me" we identify with. The true-self is the all-accepting awareness that purely *exists*.

We can perceive both of these parts of ourselves. When we think a "thought," we can hear it voiced in our heads. Sometimes we consciously make this voice happen and sometimes it occurs without our instruction, but all of these thoughts are the ego. The true-self is the awareness of our inner dialogue. In order to see the world, there must be an eyeball to see it. Likewise, in order for us to hear the ego, there must be an observer to hear it; this observer is the true-self.

These two aspects live in us and work together to create our experience of the world.

The Epic Battle between Ego and Self

> God equals Man minus Ego.
> – Sathya Sai Baba: Hindu-Muslim Guru [6]

When we lose our true-selves beneath repression, we give the ego complete control to dominate the inner-self with an iron fist; the ego holds us together throughout our self-hate.

Repression of the true-self mixed with an untrained and wild ego creates a dichotomy within: the ego maintains a false-person and the true-self is hidden. Once the true-self is covered up, it is easy for the ego to convince us that its voice is our voice, giving it total control.

We can guide the way our egos tell us to feel and act, but we seldom take the reigns and lead them. We slip into unconsciousness and let the habitual-mind run our lives for us. When we do not listen to our thoughts, we live out of compulsion as the ego tells us to.

The ego is not a "bad guy"; its decisions are instinctual. The ego keeps us alive when we live unconsciously and it is quite good at this task. However, it can become destructive if we release all decisions to the ego and lose ourselves.

An untamed ego serves its own goals first, even if they are harmful to us. When the true-self disappears deep within us, the ego gets everything it wants and this leaves it to go crazy and erratic.

The ego has no real power of its own other than what it can convince us to think and do. We ultimately make the decision of whether or not to act on what the ego recommends to us and it cannot force us to do anything. However, the ego knows its own powers of persuasion; it is an insider that we put great trust in. It is full of ideas that sound legitimate in theory and it tricks us into following it. This ability to convince us of its validity is where it gains its great strength. It is the serpent that tempts us to eat the apple from the tree, even though we know not to.

It is easy to blame the ego for our false-self and then hate it for what it has done to us, but the ego attempts to serve us in the ways that we request it to. If we create the need for a false-self, then the ego maintains it. Acting as a false-person is impossible for the true-self to do, so it becomes the ego's duty.

We use the ego to create a façade on the outside, but it is meant to be a tool for conscious creation. It is a neutral entity that gives "voice" to our true-selves. It allows us to put intention into language. When used this way, we are free to direct and co-create our lives. Instead, we use the ego to create a false-self. This is no easy feat and the ego is distracted from its other duties in the never-ending maintenance of an elaborate hoax. At this point, the ego changes from a friend and counselor to a separate creature that is in competition with us for survival. The ego then uses us to fulfill its agenda, rather than the opposite. It makes decisions to enhance it, rather than help the true-self.

This morbid role we give to the ego is destructive, but it has served us for a long time. We cannot get angry with the ego about doing a job that we assigned to it. The ego-self protects us against our own self-hate; it creates a self-inflated version of ourselves for us to believe in so that we do not realize our self-abuse and repression. This allows us to go on living, even when we carry a grotesque amount of misery within us.

The ego's controls get stronger with each aspect we repress. It creates a network of lies and fallacy that hold all repression in the subconscious without us even realizing it. These lies allow us to exist even though we repress and hate ourselves. It is a brilliant scheme and the ego deserves much gratitude for keeping us alive and functioning even when we are living in hate and fear.

> The problem I see with humanity today is we don't truly know ourselves anymore. We have the nine-to-five job, we have the house, the children, the bills, the television, the hobbies, and the errands that we run every single day, and we eventually begin to believe that this is who we are.
> – Ben Stewart: Public Speaker and Director [7]

Many of us have left the inner-self sleeping for so long that we do not even know we are asleep. We forget who we are and then identify with the ego.

Listening to our egos, rather than reacting to them, gives us conscious awareness of thoughts and allows us to recognize the ego so we can choose whether or not to act on it. With mindfulness we can make the distinction between our true-selves and our ego-selves. Once we can tell the difference between the ego and the true-self, we take back our personal power. Listening to the mind with awareness and love removes the ego's ability to run our lives.

Observing the ways we sabotage and bring unhappiness to ourselves can help us identify the ego. The destructive aspects that manifest externally are a direct reflection of the ego and internal repression. When we learn to accept all of these aspects, we start to crack the very foundation of our ego-façade, and the whole building topples down.

Self-love and self-acceptance create a safe environment for the true-self to come to the surface. When we accept ourselves, no matter what, we do not need to believe in a false-self and repression disintegrates.

A healthy relationship with the ego allows it to present ideas and options, and we can pick and choose the ones that serve us. A toxic relationship allows it to take over and serve only itself.

Ego Techniques and Tactics

> If you know others and know yourself, you
> will not be imperiled in a hundred battles.
> – Sun Tzu: 6th Century Chinese General [8]

We do not have to kill our ego in order for our true-selves to prosper. Rather, we can learn to work with it and understand it. As we each get to know our own egos, we learn how to work with them on a personal level.

The ego only requires some minor alterations to get it back on track. It is a guidance system to help us with life, but we stopped questioning the thoughts and feelings that it presented, so it is way off target.

There is a balance between the true-self and the ego that is beautiful and creative. Allow the ego to become a true friend and ally. We can do this by becoming aware of the battle tactics that the ego uses; a good knowledge of our opponent allows us to find inner peace:

Ego Labels

The ego attaches labels to us, (e.g., "I am smart," "I am a mother," "I am rich," "I am poor," etc.). As soon as we agree with the labels, the ego begins to play its constant reminder that we are these aspects.

We are not these labels, but the ego can use them to manipulate us. Holy wars are a brilliant and terrible example of this. By saying, "I am a Christian," thousands of so-called witches were burned. By saying, "I am a Muslim," suicide bombers were motivated to kill. These labels can be deeply personal and profound, but once we agree with them, the ego can twist what the label means and thereby twist who we think we are.

Labels turn our infinite-self into a flattened, stereotypical, conceptual "personality." Once we agree to this false-self, we live in a way that expresses the stagnant and unchangeable vision we believe in, even if it goes against our own logic and inner-knowing.

As we become aware of the labels the ego uses, we can intervene and stop subscribing to its ridiculous blog of radical banter. When we stop acting as the "personality" our egos choose for us, we are empowered to live as our true-selves.

Neutrality

The ego is neutral. It does not discriminate between "right" and "wrong;" there is "survival" and "non-survival." The ego thinks that becoming stronger assures survival, so it seeks ways to make itself greater. It has no bias or moral values. It uses whatever it thinks will accomplish its purposes.

We can reset the ego by listening to it. It is up to us to decide if the method the ego chooses is the one we want to use. If we hear an option it selects and decide not to do it, the ego learns not to present those types of options. The inner-self is the check-and-balance on the ego's tactics.

We train the ego just like any animal. The ego wants to make us happy and seeks approval. If it craves a treat and we indulge, it learns that craving a treat gets rewarded. If it recommends a behavior and we refuse, it is less likely to bring it up in the future. The ego only does what we train it to do.

"Mine"

A misguided ego craves the acquisition of external objects. When people become "*my* friends," "*my* spouse," or "*my* family," and objects become: "*my* house," "*my* money," or "*my* clothes," the ego is saying that *they are us*, "That is a part of *me*."

"Things" distract us from our true-selves. If we live externally and believe that objects express us into the physical world, we stop looking within for the real person. Physical objects can be changed on command and the ego uses them to define us. This tricky tactic gets us focused outside of ourselves and the ego loves the pliability of being able to change its representation of "me" as it chooses.

These are not a representation of the true-self, because they can be changed by factors outside of us. If a hurricane blows over your house, are you lost? If the economy takes a dive and you lose your fortune, are you lost? If your clothes burn in a fire, are you lost? If your spouse leaves you, are you lost? A misguided ego would have us believe that we are.

To overcome this tactic, we can let go of things, people, and attachments that belong to the ego. Since our true-self does not need anything outside of itself, virtually every "thing" is an ego belonging.

When we shed our attachments, we release the need for the ego to maintain and track them. It is not necessary to kick everything and everyone out of our lives; the goal is to release the attachment to them. The easiest way to release an attachment is by getting rid of it, but with practice and consciousness we can learn to let go regardless.

Ego Voices

The ego creates an endlessly streaming dialogue of thoughts to cover up our repressions. The more of these repetitive recordings there are, the harder it is for the true-self to get through. These ego-tapes play so much and so often that we tune them out. This is very much like the constant ringing in our ear drums. We stop hearing the sound, because it is always there. We can have hundreds of tapes playing in our heads at any given time, but we do not hear them unless we consciously listen and identify them as parts of the false-self.

The repetition of the mind berates us into submission. The mind plays the same redundant tapes over and over again until we believe them. These "voices" become so familiar that we believe they are us.

Naming the voices is a Buddhist technique that helps us distinguish ourselves from our egos. Phrases like, "I hear you, Insecurity," or "I understand you, Self-Doubt," directly address the voice. This separates it from the idea of self as well as allows us to accept that it is there. Once we know that a voice is not us, we can listen to it without attaching to it and then decide whether or not to act on it.

When we think of ego thoughts as voices, we can recognize when they come up and learn to overcome them. Our thought patterns become options, rather than instant reactions, and we become the chess master that moves pieces according to the best possible outcome. When we analyze situations with mindfulness, it is easier to decide on the option that brings ease and flow, rather than the option that enhances our pseudo-self.

Isolation

The ego encourages isolation and disconnectedness. We learn to live in our heads instead of as our true-selves. We learn to disconnect from ourselves and others, distrusting our surroundings in favor of the version of reality our minds tell us. Isolation of self stops us from pursuing all endeavors for happiness, personal growth, and expression, in favor of the ego-self.

We can overcome this separation from self by consciously spending more time alone. When we shift to living in our hearts as our true-selves, we release the need for the ego-self. This will be discussed more later.

The Ego-Voice Called Control

> When we get frightened, we want to control everything,
> and then we shut off the flow of our good. Trust life.
> Everything we need is here for us.
> – Louise L. Hay: Public Speaker and Writer [9]

Within our true-selves is a constant state of Love. When we cut off our true-selves, we stop feeling this free-flow of Love that *exists*. The ego invented the games of manipulation and control in the attempts to fulfill this perceived "lack of love."

Control is an attempt to gain approval and love through force.

When we perceive that others do not act in love toward us, we try to force them into acting ways that *seem* loving.

We have certain ideas about how people act when they are in love. If we do not see those physical actions, we believe that we are not loved. We then manipulate others into doing specific actions to convince ourselves that they love us. For example, the Jealousy Voice might believe that affection is Love. In an attempt to force our loved-one to fulfill our needs, we might demand that they cannot be with other people. In another example, the Sympathy Voice might equate pity to Love. Then we manipulate and lie to get people to feel bad for us. These forms of control attempt to acquire the actions that we believe exhibit love.

There are many ways force is used to "attain" love. A parent might yell at their child and make demands upon them in the attempt to feel respected; physical touch is used to "acquire" affection; money can be used to purchase service, which is also sign of love. Anytime control is used, we can be certain that the controller feels unloved.

Many ego voices have their roots in control. The more we love and accept ourselves, the less we have to manipulate others. We also know that when someone acts forceful toward us, it is their attempt to "attain" love. If we respond with acceptance when someone attempts to control us, their games and tactics disintegrate; we refuse to play.

We all have Love inside of us, at all times. It is a fallacy to believe that we do not have Love and that we have to acquire it.

When we acknowledge this, we empower ourselves to live in True Freedom.

We control others when we feel out of control ourselves. When we discover and know our true-selves, we find inner stability. This releases the need to manipulate others.

Love is all we Need

> How rare are those who…look within their bodies, into their minds. Through loving devotion, their ego evaporates.
> – *Guru Granth Sahib*: Text of Sikhism [10]

We can understand and find peace with our egos in a play-by-play game of wits, but it is a lot of work. We spend a long time building up our "personality," (a great label of the ego,) and it can take a long time to break it down, brick by brick. Though this method does work and it is useful to learn as we grow and develop.

The root cause of ego voices is repression; we can unravel the false-self by accepting our true-selves as we *are*. Once we love our true-selves, the ego no longer needs to prove life is any different than it *is*; the tapes stop on their own. When we do not need the ego to defend us, it is free to create.

The more we understand ourselves and our egos, the more we can understand and love others. The ego is quite clever. When we learn to see its tricks within ourselves, it is easy to see them in others. As we clear up our own ego-games, we can stop playing everyone else's as well. The ego shifts back into its wonderful role as an advisor. Carl Jung said:

> Knowing your own darkness is the best method for dealing with the darkness of other people. [11]

Unconditional acceptance silences *all* voices. When we clean up the ego through acceptance, it becomes a tool for our heart's desires. The ego is a friend that is full of awesome and terrible ideas. Hinduism views the ego as a serpent that, once mastered, can be worn around the neck as an adornment. We want to hear the thoughts as they arise, without judging them, and then let them go.

Many of us have used the ego for destructive purposes and defense mechanisms for so long that it has become quite dark. As we silence the habitual thoughts of the ego, we put ourselves back in the driver seat and take an active role in our own lives again.

Practice!

1. Meditation and self-love free us from the ego.
2. Listen for the thoughts that rest below the thoughts. These are your subconscious coming through. Do not be upset if they are uncomfortable; forgive and accept them.
3. Naming "voices" can help us accept them without identifying with them. There are many possibilities for voices, here are some I have experienced:
   Self-Hate, Vanity, Approval, Self-Inflation, Self-Doubt, Fear, Worry, Stress, Control, Suffering/Pain Body, [12]

Desire, Addiction, Guilt, Obsession, Anger, Sloth, Procrastination, Loneliness, Jealousy, etc.
4. Get rid of useless stuff. Stuff belongs to the ego.
5. Make a list of the labels you identify with. These are made up. Strive to detach from all of them. You are a being of infinite potential and possibilities. Stop confining yourself to a false, two-dimensional person.

    NOTE: Even the labels you think are positive can restrict or limit you. If you say, "I am beautiful," does that mean you must always be beautiful, no matter the cost? What does "beautiful" mean? Does it change?
6. When people attack you, let them win the argument. The ego is enraged by losing because its control over us and others is diminished. Forgive people for their abuse and let it go.
7. **Questions:**

    What is "human nature"?

    Who are *you*? Where do *you* go when you sleep?

    Is Love compatible with ego?

3. FEAR

> The only thing we have to fear is fear itself.
> – Franklin D. Roosevelt: President of the USA [1]

As we learn to love ourselves and quiet the ego mind, fear complicates the equation. Fear can trump consciousness and willpower, causing detrimental effects. Fear is a mind-body connection that is immediate and overwhelming. When its claws take hold, it can dictate our every move with little resistance. A phobia can convince us to disregard all logic and do the opposite of what we want to do.

The purpose of fear is to initiate the fight or flight response. This physical reaction to a mental stimulus can be life-saving. The ability to perceive a threat and then increase physical capabilities as a direct result has no-doubt saved many creatures. When an external source threatens our lives, nothing is more important to us than survival. Our bodies are designed around this concept. When in danger, every part of our beings is rerouted and dedicated to escaping or eliminating the source of fear.

Fear is useful in situations that require an increase in adrenaline; it is when our fears become irrational and excessive that they lead to destructive behavior. For example, the fear of loud noises may cause us to jump at a gunshot; this is helpful for starting a race or escaping an attacker. If the fear of loud noises causes us to run away whenever someone yells at us, it is unhelpful. Fears and phobias that do not require adrenaline production inhibit our life experience.

The chemicals released during fear modify how the body functions. Fear is meant to be a strong and all-encompassing force because our survival can depend on the ability of fear to motivate us! When we experience fear, the body's adrenal glands start pumping epinephrine (adrenaline), which results in rapid heart rate, increased blood pressure, tightening of muscles, sharpened or redirected senses, dilation of the pupils, and blocked pain receptors. These body reactions allow us to function at the peak of our abilities for a limited amount of time.

Fear also affects the mind. Deadly situations require us to make split second decisions in order to escape or defeat any attacker we face. If we need to run away from a bear, we do not have time to decide where to go: we need to respond instantly to the situation as it occurs. This means that when we operate from a place of fear, there is a tendency to act in knee-jerk reactions, without logic and reason. Fear-based decisions use instincts and do not necessarily promote joy, love, and happiness.

Many of us hold on to fear for extended periods. Prolonged production of adrenaline leads to: palpitations, accelerated heart, abnormal electrical heart activity, anxiety, headaches, tremors, hypertension, chronic stress, immune deficiency, heart failure, and heart attack. [2] The very symptoms that save us in a dangerous situation can kill us if they linger too long.

Our different emotional states are useful for different situations and a healthy body knows when, where, and how to use them, but we are often ruled by our minds and our emotions get out of hand, causing immense suffering for ourselves and others.

Fear versus Love

> I believe that every single event in life happens in an opportunity to choose love over fear.
> – Oprah Winfrey: Talk-Show Host [3]

Love and fear are our two main motivating forces. We either want more of something or we want less. Love draws us closer to a certain person, place, or thing, while fear repels us from them.

Our other emotions branch out of either love or fear. In love (acceptance), we experience joy, trust, pleasure, arousal, curiosity, gratitude, peace, and happiness. In fear (non-acceptance), we feel sadness, anger, anxiety, hatred, jealousy, prejudice, greed, and paranoia. Our emotions are tactics to either draw something toward us or push it away.

Many qualities of the mind and body change based off of whether we are experiencing love or fear. According to

Dr. Bruce Lipton, we cannot experience these two states at the same time. When we experience fear, the blood in our viscera (gut) is redirected to the appendages; in this state we are unable to grow, but we are ready to fight. When we are in love, the blood stays in the gut, enabling us to grow. [4] Our bodies themselves are changed by our emotions.

Love encourages us to grow, while fear discourages us. If we love ourselves, we want more of ourselves. If we fear ourselves, we want less. Love leads to freedom and expression of the self, while fear leads to restriction and repression.

We cannot love and accept when we operate out of a place of fear. Often fear is brought on because we perceive that there is not enough love and this flips us into survival mode. When we realize that there is an infinite source of Love within us, fear disintegrates.

The world's great teachers have shown us that fear is not the way to reach a state of Love. Transcending fear is a universal concept in our major religions:

> **Christianity:** The Bible says in 1 John: "God is love. Whoever lives in love lives in God, and God in him… There is no fear in love. But perfect love drives out fear, because fear has to do with punishment. The one who fears is not made perfect in love." [5]
>
> **Judaism:** The Jewish Torah and the Christian Bible both periodically say we should fear God, but this refers to awe and respect, not the physical state of fear. The English word "fear" is a translation for two Hebrew words: *yirah* (piety and reverence), and *pachad* (terrified dread). [6] *Yirah* is used in reference to God.

Islam: The Quran says, "Whoever submits his whole self to God and is a doer of good, he will get his reward with his Lord; on such shall be no fear, nor shall they grieve." [7] When one submits to Allah, there is no fear; Allah is an absence of fear.

Hinduism: Hindus say that the True Self can be found with the release of fear. The Hindu god, Brahman, says, "Released from greed, fear, anger, absorbed in Me and made pure by the practice of wisdom, many have attained My own state of being." [8]

Buddhism: Siddhartha Gautama said, "Look within. Be still. Free from fear and attachment, know the sweet joy of the way." [9] Our inner-selves are free from fear.

Love above Fear

> Nothing in life is to be feared, it is only to be understood. Now is the time to understand more, so that we may fear less.
> – Marie Curie: Nobel Prize in Physics and Chemistry [10]

We are seldom taught how to understand and work with fear. We worry incessantly and "deal with it," instead of growing from it. We fear sources that are not even life threatening. We make up fears, we inherit fears, we worry, and then we let these mind-states run wild. For example, the fear of public speaking (the most common fear) can lead to shaky voice, increased sweating, and inability to focus. These effects hinder the ability to speak!

The more fears we have, the longer and more frequently we find ourselves in an unhealthy state of being. We worry for friends, we worry for family, we worry about our jobs, we worry about the time, and we worry about ourselves. When we feel stress, epinephrine is at work in our bodies for an extended period of time. Extended periods of stress and worry have been linked to chronic diseases and shortened lifespan. [11] The longer we let our fears have free reign inside of us, the less happy and healthy we are.

We try to convince ourselves that we worry out of love, but worry does not do anything. If we can help a person, then we do it. Worry only hurts us. Siddhartha Gautama said, "What benefit is there in being frightened and scared of what is unalterable?" [12] Worry is an unjustifiable fear that can last for years on end if we let it.

For most of us, fear is unnecessary. Our lives rarely get threatened and we seldom need adrenaline production. Logic and reasoning can replace fear in most situations. Fear can stop us from putting our hand in a fire, but so will common sense, knowledge, and pain receptors. Limiting our fears to situations where we need adrenaline production leaves our hearts and minds clear.

Fear is nothing more than an attachment: we attach to a person, place, thing, or idea and fear losing it, or we attach to something that is not present. There is no fear if we are unconditionally accepting. Fear is what we experience when we are attached to something outside of ourselves and we are afraid of losing it. Even the fear of death is an attachment to the physical body. Releasing attachments to external objects causes fear to fall away.

As long as we have fears, we cannot accept ourselves, because we fear existence as it *is* and who we really *are*. However, instead of fixating on fear and thereby empowering it, we can shift our attention to love and acceptance. Love drives out fear. When we come to ourselves with love and compassion, we are in a place to transcend and work with our fears.

Fear is a deep-rooted force and it requires the utmost understanding and forgiveness in order to work with it. Once we find solidity within ourselves through acceptance, we can start addressing fears on a more individual level. Most fears develop in traumatic and upsetting ways, (past trauma, repression, learned behaviors, etc.), so working with them requires a strong stability of self and a foundation of Love. Once we have found Love within, we can figure out where our individual fears come from and confront them.

Understanding and acceptance dissolve fears. When we love what we are afraid of, and love the fact that we are afraid, the feeling disappears. Learning to love that which we fear helps us transcend it.

There is an African parable that helps us understand how to work with fear:

> When lions hunt on the savanna, they divide into two groups. The stronger group hides on one side of the prey. The weaker group goes to the other side and growls as loudly as possible. The prey runs from the roar and their escape leads them right into the strong group's trap.

This story reveals that fear drives us into further hardship. Remember, in a time of terror, run toward the lion's roar!

Fears are aspects of the ego. The true-self is an all-accepting awareness that just observes; there is no fear. This means that we can work with fears the same way we work with the ego. Once we stop identifying with our fears, we choose whether or not to act on them. Through naming our fears, we address and confront them in a safe way. Facing fears alleviates them.

When we feel afraid, we can listen to the fear and embrace it as an aspect of ourselves. Love fear! By loving and accepting our fears, we realize they are irrational to begin with and they fall away on their own. Fear has many faces, but all can be healed through love and acceptance.

Fear is an excellent clue into our own minds. Each fear can be traced to something that we refuse to accept. Our fears are tied to our very survival instincts themselves, the most basic form of instinct. [13] We can understand ourselves by addressing phobias and acknowledging how we feel about them. This gives us the freedom to let go. Even the most disturbing fears can be healed with love; the darkest room can be lit with a candle. When we accept that a fear is present, we can learn to transcend it.

Discovering the roots of fears and addressing them can be difficult. We unconsciously repress situations that led to fear or we repress the feeling that caused the fear in the first place. When working with fear, use logic and reasoning in what is safe for you. Fears are delicate. Use caution when working with extreme phobias, but do not fear fear itself. Fear can be addressed and healed with dedication and steady practice. For most of us, fear can be conquered on our own, but some may want the assistance of a professional.

Remember that our fears are not us. A misguided ego is very afraid; it is always in survival mode, believing that it is dying. Fear is an instinct that is necessary if we live unconsciously because it protects us from harm. *Consciousness eliminates the need for fear.*

As we address our fears, we become free to act in the ways that we choose, rather than the ways we need to. Through direct confrontation, we realize there is no cause to fear in the first place. Facing our fears changes us on a fundamental level because they embed themselves deep, profoundly affecting our actions. Overcoming our fears, and the experience of fear itself, is a challenge that we all face in the process of re-discovering ourselves.

Practice!

1. Find safe ways to challenge your fears.
2. When you experience fear, meditate for ten minutes. Focus on your breathing and listen to the voice with mindfulness.
3. Love fear and the sources of fear. This may seem impossible, but there is always a way. Fear is a powerful teacher.
4. We fear what we do not understand, so listen to yourself. Fears exist for a reason. Release the fear when you are ready.
5. **Questions:**
   What is fear?
   Where does fear come from?
   Is it possible to transcend fear completely?

4. SUFFERING

> Much of your pain is self-chosen. It is the bitter
> potion by which the physician within you heals
> your sick self. Therefore trust the physician, and
> drink his remedy in silence and tranquility.
> – Kahlil Gibran: Poet and Writer [1]

Rough patches on the road of life are often unavoidable and unchangeable, but our perspective on these difficult parts is our choice. However, rather than deal with potholes as they come, we re-route our entire lives to avoid a few dings in the road. We choose how to feel about all that happens, but we unconsciously select perspectives that lead to unhappiness and pain.

External stimuli impact us because we let them; we live in a reactionary state and do not pay attention to our surroundings. In this state, we do not make a choice about what our perspective is; the ego selects it for us. Consciousness gives us awareness of moments as they occur so we can choose actions that create happiness.

Many of us have the habit of living in suffering and pain. These are only behavioral patterns and we can retrain all of our habits with practice. Happiness is something we choose, it does not simply *happen* to us.

> I have found that most people are about as
> happy as they make up their minds to be.
> – Abraham Lincoln: President of the USA [2]

When we suffer, we can either change it or we cannot. Regardless, if we direct our energy to dwelling on the pain, then we are helpless to change it. If all energy is used up in complaining, we do not have the energy to take action. If we deplete ourselves by focusing on the hardships, we do not have the energy to be happy.

We suffer because we choose to. This also means that we can *not suffer* because we choose to. We each have the capability to decide our own emotions. No one gives us an emotion. If you have ever tried to console someone who is sad, you can understand this. No matter how hard we want to make someone feel happy, it is up to them to decide.

We choose suffering because that is what we know. It is a familiar way to teach ourselves important life lessons. Suffering is a tricky game that is easy to get sucked into, but there are small shifts that make it easier to choose happiness:

Lifestyle Choices: Our lifestyle choices impact how our bodies and brains function. The brain produces over fifty known active drugs: amino acids, vitamins, minerals. The chemicals we ingest and create form into neurotransmitters that affect our moods.[3] We can alter our emotions and state of being through diet, exercise, and sleeping habits. Healthy people are happy people.

Find the Virus: In our culture, we fixate on taking a pill or finding that "miracle cure." We want drugs to fix the symptoms instead of discovering the initial cause ourselves. In the long run, many of these so-called fixes make us worse than we were without them. This applies to literal and metaphorical viruses and can impact us on physical, mental, emotional, or spiritual levels.

Productive Habits: The neural pathways in the brain form habits; they get used to firing in certain ways and get stuck in them. The more we think one way, the stronger the pathway becomes. The more we walk on a set path, the deeper the grooves get. When we repeatedly experience suffering, our neural pathways lead us in that direction. When we shift to happiness and love, they become easier as well.

The reason we suffer is because we choose to suffer. There is some degree of suffering that we cannot change, like sickness and death, but even with these forms of suffering we can change our perspective on them.

In any given situation, there are many possible perspectives that we can take. We can view the glass as half-full or half-empty, but it does not change the amount of water in the glass. The situation stays the same, but we choose how to view it and how that view affects us. For example, death is a cause for extreme mourning in some cultures, while others celebrate it (e.g., the Mexican "Day of the Dead"). Our perspective on a situation changes how we experience it.

Outside factors affect our mood because we let them. Though few admit it, we want to suffer, and that is why we do. For example, we watch suffering in movies for entertainment, we make unhealthy lifestyle choices that lead to misery, and we dwell in suffering rather than forgive or correct a situation. We love to hold on to our suffering.

Suffering is a habit. Overcoming depression, self-sabotage, and pain is a matter of retraining our brains. Yet, one in 10 people in the United States take anti-depressants to solve unhappiness,[4] though 70 percent do not need them.[5] For most of us, we want to suffer and we choose to suffer, so that becomes the habit we attach to. We chose to suffer in the past and thereby set up neural pathways to continue our suffering. We can break this chain by consciously changing our reaction to a situation in the present moment.

We form a set of unconscious reactions through social and personal conditioning, but all of this "programming" is moldable. Each time we consciously choose to stop suffering and depression, we reinforce a different neural pathway. How we feel Now is a conscious choice, and the more we choose certain emotions, the easier they become.

All major religions recognize that we suffer and most address the question of why.[6] We understand that suffering is a part of life, but we are not convinced that it is *part of us*. Each religion addresses the causes and reasons for suffering in their own way:

Buddhism: The Second Noble Truth claims that suffering is caused by ignorance and desire. [7] Suffering is caused because we either misperceived a situation or because we desired something that we did not get. The Noble Eightfold Path is a process for transcending attachment and suffering.

Hinduism: The Higher Self, Atman, is free from suffering; pain is just a result of our spiritual development and our mistakes: Karma. When we transcend Karma, we escape suffering and return to our original state.

Christianity: In the Bible, Job struggles in physical and emotional suffering, but he maintains his love and faith in God throughout. From Job's story we learn that suffering is a part of life, good things do not always happen to good people and bad things do not always happen to bad people. God is the judge and decides everything; we all experience suffering in some capacity, no matter how well we live our lives.

Islam: Islam views that we should submit ourselves to Allah/God completely. The name "Islam" is derived from the root word meaning "surrender" or "submission." Though human nature is essentially good, Muslims believe that we forget this goodness. Through submission to Allah, the world reveals itself as a beautiful creation. The Quran is a guide to proper action so that we may overcome suffering and goodness prevails. [8]

The Suffering Voice

> Success is getting what you want.
> Happiness is wanting what you get.
> – Susan Gregg: Writer and Mystic [9]

Suffering directly relates to attachment. When we attach to a certain result, we create a need in our minds for it. When these needs are not satisfied, we create suffering because of the lack of having them. A release of attachment to specific results, and a shift in perspective to acceptance, allows us to overcome suffering.

The ego attaches to suffering as a method to acquire attention and love. When we are unhappy, people act lovingly toward us and give us the attention we desire. When a baby cries, we rush to their side; when they are silent, we ignore them. These types of reactions train us to think that suffering brings love. Once the ego realizes that suffering can be used for this tactic, it attaches suffering to a part of "who we are."

The Suffering Voice of the ego often takes the role of The Victim or The Hero. Concepts like "Murphy's Law," "Bad things happen in threes," or "bad luck" can all be attributed to playing the role of The Victim or The Hero:

The Victim: When we play the role of The Victim, we are not responsible for our lives and blame external sources for anything that happens. When we put ourselves as The Victim, we take all responsibility for unhappiness off of ourselves. The Victim is sure that, "Bad things just happen to me," or "Everyone is out to get me," or even, "I did not do anything wrong!" These statements allow us to perpetuate continual suffering with no personal responsibility. There is no way to stop the suffering of The Victim, because it is caused by "someone else."

The Hero: When we play the role of The Hero, we believe we are saving the world and there is no way that we could be mistaken. We refuse to admit our flaws and unknowingly hurt other people. We cause suffering, but refuse to see that we did it. We do not see the relationship of cause and effect and what our role in perpetuating the suffering was. The Hero loves suffering, because they get to "save the world," "solve the world's problems," and "hold the world on their shoulders." The Hero is the "good guy" defeating the "bad guy." The Hero seeks out suffering, because it gives them a purpose in life.

The ego fights to prove our suffering, and our suffering validates the ego. When we act as The Victim, The Hero, or any other suffering role, we attach to pain and seek to create it more.

Suffering locks into our ego and they validate, provoke, and accentuate each other. When we release the need to play these roles, we allow ourselves to live in ease and flow, living each moment as it occurs, and seeing situations for what they *are*.

Healing the Suffering Virus

> A man who is master of himself can end a sorrow
> as easily as he can invent a pleasure. I don't want to
> be at the mercy of my emotions. I want to use them,
> to enjoy them, and to dominate them.
> – Oscar Wilde: Poet and Writer [10]

Experiencing emotions through the ego is damaging, but that is the only method that many of us know: we learn to either repress our emotions or unleash them upon innocent bystanders. This causes emotions to go unresolved within us, because we do not know how to experience them and release them. If we do not express ourselves in a healthy way, suffering inserts itself into our lives in order to solve situations on the outside that we are unable to solve on the inside.

In any given situation, there are four primary ways to deal with our emotions. When suffering arises, remember the four R's: Repress, React, Release, or Rise Above.

Repress

We are told to "Suck it up," "Walk it off," or "Be a man." We inherently understand that we cannot walk around as an emotional wreck, so we stuff our emotions deep inside and hide from them. This causes feelings to slip into our unconscious mind to be dealt with and processed by the ego. Repressed emotions do not disappear; they come back out in one way or another.

Freud explained that we experience transference of emotions from one person to another as a way to resolve them. This forces us to live in the present situations that happened in the past. [11] For example, we might transfer the anger at our father onto the middle-aged store clerk. In a sense, we become psychologically addicted to the situation or experience that hurt us and then attempt to make it happen over and over again until we deal with it.

Repressed emotions also come out through projection. Psychological projection is when we believe that others are the source of an attribute, thought, or emotion that comes from us. Built up emotions eventually pass a threshold where we cannot hold them in any longer. When this happens, we search for "reasons" to feel the way that we do. Even if we find a situation to relieve our inner tension, it is temporary and we go right back to repressing.

React

Sometimes we react to strong emotions without thinking and attempt to unload the feelings onto someone else. Hysterics, complaining, yelling, screaming, and abuse are all examples of reacting to our suffering.

Reacting to an emotion does not resolve it. There is an underlying suffering within us that caused the emotion, and if we react to external sources for it, then we never resolve the real root of the feeling within.

Losing ourselves to an emotional tantrum lets the ego control us and do as it chooses. Once the ego learns it can use emotion to get what it wants, it finds ways to bring them up in the future, even if we do not feel this way anymore.

Emotions are overwhelming and the ego loves using them to control us. If the ego knows it can use our powerful emotions to get what it desires, we experience them every time it wants something.

Release

Release finds a healthy way to let go of the emotion once we have experienced it. Instead of using the ego's twisted method to express pain, we acknowledge feelings and find an outlet for them that does not lead to more suffering. Sometimes passion can help us write a song, make a speech, or gain momentum to change. Sadness can help us make a painting, provoke personal growth, or feel compassion. These can be helpful if done with consciousness.

Sometimes conscious experience of our emotions feels weak and humbling, which enrages the ego, because it wants to use emotions to gain power and control. However, letting ourselves fully understand the causes and sources of internal suffering alleviates them. When we experience our emotions in consciousness, we can find constructive ways to express ourselves that lead to creation and resolution, rather than destruction and repression.

Rise Above

Ideally, we want to rise above suffering. We want to notice our feelings and emotions as or before they occur and make a choice about them. As we learn to be present with our emotions and experience them with consciousness, rising above them becomes enjoyable and fun.

At first, we may only realize we are wrapped up in a cycle of suffering when we have gotten in deep. With awareness, we start to hear the emotions creeping up on us before they have the chance to get their claws into our rational minds. Then we can let them go, while they are still *options* in the ego. This is the ultimate goal.

Healthy Waves of Emotion

> Don't let's forget that the little emotions
> are the great captains of our lives, and
> that we obey them without knowing it.
> – Vincent van Gogh: Painter [12]

Many of us live our lives through reaction or repression techniques. Emotional tension from the past builds up inside of us, running our lives and dictating what we do on a daily basis. Be patient with yourself as you learn to release emotional baggage. We do not want to be upset with ourselves for feeling emotions. Rather, accept that we feel the way we do and figure out the best way to proceed from there. Conscious emotions lead us to let go of all the suffering.

Learning to express emotions in a healthy way is part of maturity and it can be very difficult. Children fly off the handle in minute situations. As we grow up, we realize that yelling and screaming seldom solve the situation. (Well, sometimes we learn this.) Experiencing an emotion in consciousness allows us to understand ourselves and our feelings, which causes them to resolve in the conscious mind and dissolve themselves.

Rising above our emotions is just another way of saying "accept." We accept what is happening inside of us, understand ourselves, and acknowledge what caused the excitement. This allows the emotion to figure itself out and disappear. Acceptance is the key to overcoming suffering. Accepting ourselves and our emotions stops us from damming up emotions within and allows us to choose what to do instead of reacting in unconsciousness.

Emotions are not "good" or "bad." They are chemical reactions in the brain. We label some emotions as "bad" because we do not want to feel that way, while claiming other emotions are "good" because we want to feel that way.

When we release our attachment to specific emotions, we can experience them through acceptance and love. Releasing the need to feel a specific emotion frees us to observe and experience our emotions as they arise. When we remain conscious throughout this process, we feel our emotions without being slaves to them. Rather than trying to be happy when we are sad, we can listen to the sadness and accept it until it passes. Refusing to accept our current state causes prolonged suffering. Instead, we can let emotions soak in and feel them fully, listening to our emotional thoughts as they arise. We do not want to fall under their spell; just listen as a kind friend listens to another.

Emotions are a very powerful state to be in and we have trouble refusing to participate in the games they recommend to us. Acceptance allows us to hear and experience the emotion, without having a reaction to it. This prevents repression and allows release.

When we notice that an emotion has gotten a hold of us, we can take a few minutes to gain consciousness again, listening to the emotion until it burns itself out. Eventually, it gets tired of ranting and silences itself. There is a tendency with sadness and suffering to want to sulk and stay sad forever. Listen to your upset ego until it is done with its tantrum, then release the emotion.

Emotions are a decision we make in the present moment and how we choose to handle them is up to us. When we are slaves to our emotional states, our egos decide how our energy is used. When we rise above our suffering, we can use this energy in creative ways that lead to the advancement of ourselves and humanity.

> "When there is an ending of sorrow in yourself as a human being, then out of that comes wisdom. And when a human being transforms himself, when *you* transform yourself radically, you are affecting the whole consciousness of mankind."
>
> - J. Krishnamurti: Writer and Public Speaker [13]

Practice!

1. Find a method for self-therapy that can release blocked up emotions. There are free online manuals and tutorials for Emotional Freedom Technique (EFT) by Gary Craig. This method has been supported by Deepak Chopra, who stated, "EFT offers great healing benefits." [14] Give it a shot. If it does not serve you, find a method that does. Perhaps talking

through your personal traumas into a mirror will help. The goal is to find a healthy way to alleviate emotional blockages.
2. Write down your three favorite emotions. Now, write down your three most common emotions. If these two lists are different, you are deceiving yourself. The emotions you choose to feel the most are your favorite.
3. Accept and listen to the Suffering Voice until it fades.
4. Make a list of past events and wounds that you hold on to. Forgive yourself and others. Burn the paper.
5. **Questions:**

    What is suffering?

    Why do we suffer?

    Can we rise above suffering entirely?

5. DESIRE

> When all your desires are distilled, you will cast just
> two votes: to love more, and to be happy.
> — Hafiz: 14th Century Sufi Poet [1]

Desire is a natural part of life: our bodies have requirements to stay healthy, our minds crave stimulation, and we require a certain level of connectedness and community. The complications arise when our wants and needs start to run our lives for us.

There are many desires going on within us and we learn that they are all "bad." Yet, our desires exist for specific purposes. We get confused because we are not taught how to understand and work with them. We do not know which desires to act on and how to overcome them naturally. We lose ourselves to unconscious desires and either feed them endlessly or attempt to repress them away.

Desire helps us maintain a healthy balance, but it gets hijacked by the ego when unmanaged. As we understand and befriend our egos, we want to understand desire as well.

Desire comes in two primary forms:

Need: A need is immediately essential to our continued existence. If a need is not fulfilled, we perish or go insane. Need is tied to our survival, it has a sense of urgency, and it is one of the most basic forms of instinct.

Want: A want is something that we would like to have, but we will live without it. We might choose to be unhappy if we do not get what we want, but we do not require it. This is a leisurely longing that can be satisfied when it is available.

The ego understands the difference between these two cravings: it knows needs are always satisfied before wants. In order to manipulate us, a misguided ego might then re-label "wants" into "needs" to get what it desires.

Once we create a "need," we believe we *must* have it and that we will die if we do not get it, even if that is not that case. For example, if I *want* to help a friend and I also *want* a television, there is no sense of urgency and I can choose which is more important. If I *need* a new television and I only *want* to help a friend, then I will choose the television because my survival depends on it. This logically does not make sense, but to the ego, needs must be satisfied at all costs.

There are very few cases where we "need." Obesity rates have made heart disease the leading cause of death in the United States. [2] This means that *not* having food is a need for some! The needs that must be fulfilled for the human organism to continue living are very minimal. Long-term fasting has been used in religious and personal growth for thousands of years and has been linked to longevity and extended life. [3] Most "needs" are misclassified ego wants.

The brain does not know the difference between a real-need and an imagined-need. The mind and body only understand "need." There are not varying levels of need. If we say, "I need that television," our mind-body believes that we will die without it. This links the needed item to our survival and creates a sense of fear within us that does not get resolved until we acquire the "need."

Wants are *options*, while needs are *requirements*. Few of us can say we need anything; appropriately identifying our desires makes them easier to overcome. Shifting our perspective from "needs" to "wants" takes our desires out of the "must satisfy" category, and we can make a conscious choice about which desires to pursue.

Guilty Pleasures

> Oftentimes in denying yourself pleasure you do but store
> the desire in the recesses of your being. Who knows but
> that which seems omitted today, waits for tomorrow?
> – Kahlil Gibran: Poet and Writer [4]

There is a whole line of self-hatred associated with wants. We learn that we cannot have all that we desire and we should be ashamed for wanting in the first place. This leads to a whole bunch of ego games in our attempt to acquire more and then cover up our guilt over it.

Guilt is a red flag for self-hate. Guilt means that we do not accept what is happening and feel ashamed in some way. For many of us, our desires are a whole realm of reasons to hate ourselves and others. When someone buys a lot of things, we label them as "extravagant," "flashy," and "shallow" to justify that there is something "wrong" with them. Meanwhile, our own wants are labeled "sinful" and "shameful," and we are "worthless" because we want them.

Nearly all we crave is a want, especially in a world where all of our needs are constantly met. In a moment where we are satiated, there is no reason why wanting food is more practical than wanting a car. We do not need either of them, so they are equal in that moment.

There is no logical reason for guilt; everyone has desires. The world restricts us, so we long for more. This wanting comes from the desire to experience more and become more. It is the body and mind's natural way of asking for what they require. This is not "bad." We require certain goods for our survival and desire is a mechanism that the mind and body set up to make sure we get them.

We all just want to be at peace with ourselves and the world we live in. The random and exaggerated cravings we have are an attempt to meet those goals. Most desires are an attempt to get attention, affection, appreciation, and acceptance, which Deepak Chopra distinguishes as our four basic needs. [5]

We see objects and experiences and we crave them; that is a healthy part of a curious mind. The problems arise from the attempts to fulfill our desires. It is the unbridled control of the ego that leads to a caravan of cravings racing toward a cliff of self-destruction.

If we believe our desires are "wrong," we must repress them and deny ourselves the joys of living in this beautiful world. However, some of our desires spread love and happiness. For example, the desire to share experiences creates culture and community. Some desires can help us and others, if we know when to act on them.

Repressing desires does not make them disappear. Ignored desires sit in the subconscious, often warping perverse qualities, until we force them out of us. Repressed desires can become more grotesque than they were in the first place. If we repress the desire to eat, we may find ourselves craving enormous amounts of food. If we repress sexual desires, we find movies overrun with sex and lust. We have natural instincts that cause us to desire; repression does not solve them.

The more we hate a want, the more we hate ourselves for wanting. Once we hate ourselves for wanting, we find ourselves wanting the "forbidden fruit" even more! This is not an effective method for working with our true-selves. When you hear, "Do not think about a Pink Elephant," what are you now thinking about? When a smoker hears, "You should not smoke," they hear "smoke" and crave a cigarette. Repression causes us to fixate on what we want and thereby crave it more.

> It's important to live the wantings as they come
> and not get stuck somewhere, stagnant.
> – Rumi: 13th Century Sufi Poet [6]

If we hide from our wants, it is difficult to attain them. Hiding from our desires confuses us and we have no natural drive to do anything. We get confused as to what we do and why, lose track of what we want, attempt to satisfy feelings that we do not understand, and forget how to voice our needs. This leads to aggravation, frustration, empty wandering, and miscommunication. We believe that people should just know what we want, but they cannot know if we do not know ourselves.

Repressing, dismissing, and refusing to accept desire stems from self-hate and lack of understanding. Instead, we want to listen and accept desires, without attaching to them, and make a conscious choice on how to fulfill them, if we so choose. Oftentimes, it is enough to admit that we want something and let it go. Other times, we can form goals and ambitions about how to proceed. Either way, the habit of working *with* desires rather than *against* them helps us move forward in ways that promote growth and happiness for all.

Ego-Desire versus Heart-Desire

> The heart's earnest and pure desire is always fulfilled.
> In my own experience I have often seen this rule verified.
> Service of the poor has been my heart's desire, and
> it has always thrown me amongst the poor and
> enabled me to identify myself with them.
> – Mahatma Gandhi: Activist [7]

An unhealthy ego longs to become bigger, better, and stronger. Wants of the ego come back to becoming "The Best" (extreme amounts of money, fame, glamour, power, etc.). These wants are not worth pursuing, because even if we attain these extreme goals, they do not make us happy. We have to be The Best in all situations before the ego is satisfied and that is impossible. Even if we do acquire the extreme desires of the ego, we then look toward what we do not have.

Our true-selves do not want what the ego craves. For example, an untamed ego may want to be a famous musician, seeking to be stronger and better than others, while the true-self wants to create music. In this situation, true happiness comes from pursuing music out of a love of creation. This comes from a place of love, rather than from a place of self-hate (i.e., I am not good enough; if I was famous then everyone would love me and I could influence many.)

The ego recognizes heart-desires and then uses them to get what it wants: power, fame, fortune, etc. If we trace our cravings back to the original heart-desire, we can discover what our true-selves want and the initial root of that desire. In the previous example, if we desire to be a famous musician, perhaps the heart-desire is to have music be a regular part of our lives.

A heart-desire can always be satisfied. When we learn to accept wants and then release them, we are free to do and be what we love for the pure joy of it.

We can recognize desires of the true-self because they lead to the spread of happiness and love in the world. It is easy to achieve our heart-desires, because they bring joy to everyone. It is difficult to achieve ego-desires, because they attempt to diminish others, so they meet with resistance and tension. The heart's true desires help us to create, spread love, and form ambitions. The true-self desires personal growth and world growth, while the corrupt ego desires destruction of others to make it look bigger.

When we understand our desires, they can be a cause for passion and burn for life; we discover our purpose. There is no reason to feel guilty for any desires, they are clues to our true-selves and why we are here. Tamed and understood desires can cause a thirst for life that leads to a rich feeling of fulfillment.

We can listen to desires and distinguish whether they are ego-wants or heart-wants. Once we discover a desire of the heart, we can work toward it with dedication, persistence, and diligence. Oftentimes people flock to us to help with our heart-desires. There is a brilliant radiance that comes from people living from their hearts and others want to join in that. When we act from this place in ourselves, people sense our genuine nature and the love we exude is contagious.

There is no shame in *any* desire, but we can feel free to act on desires of the heart without reserve, knowing that they lead to the happiness of everyone.

Overcoming Unhelpful Desires

> If you desire many things, many
> things will seem but a few.
> – Benjamin Franklin: Inventor and Writer [8]

The paths we take in the pursuit of wants lead to suffering. The major religions teach that unbridled desires can cause devastation and pain:

Buddhism: The Four Noble Truths explain desire and ignorance as the causes for all suffering.

Islam: The Quran teaches us not to make desire into a god: "Do you see such a one as takes as his god his own vain desire? God has, knowing left him astray, and sealed his hearing and his heart, and put a cover on his sight." [9]

Hinduism: The Bhagavad Gita says, "This is the soul-destroying threefold entrance to hell: desire, anger, and greed. Every man should avoid them." [10]

Christianity: The Bible explains, "You want something but don't get it. You kill and covet, but you cannot have what you want. You quarrel and fight. You do not have, because you do not ask God. When you ask, you do not receive, because you ask with wrong motives, that you may spend what you get on your pleasures." [11]

It is obvious that desires can be destructive, but ignoring them is not helpful to anyone. Repressing them does not alleviate them. Ideally we could rise above them, but this requires a high level of consciousness and maturity that many of us struggle with.

At the point we feel desire, it is too late to transcend it; we have already felt it and trying to avoid the desire leads to repression. The same religious texts that condemn the pursuit of desires also advise how to overcome them:

Islam: The pursuit of desires is foolish, since Allah decides all. "God enlarges the sustenance which He gives to whichever of

His servants He pleases; and He similarly grants by strict measure, as He pleases: for God has full knowledge of all things." [12]

Christianity: Surrender desires to God to release them. "Ask and it will be given to you; seek and you will find; knock and the door will be opened to you." [13]

Neither Islam nor Christianity say to ignore desires. Rather, it is quite worthless to seek them when it is God that has the power to fulfill them. We can instead acknowledge a want and then surrender control of it to a Higher Power. It is fine to have the desire; it is the pursuit of desire that causes unhappiness. Desire is an infamous fish; catch it and release it to a Supreme Being. "Let go and let God."

The Eastern religions have another way to work with desire:

Hinduism: The pursuit of pleasure, kama, is a legitimate purpose for life, but the ultimate goal is to overcome Karma [14] and achieve a higher level of existence. The repression of desire can be worse than seeking the desires in the first place.

Buddhism: The *attachment* to desires leads to suffering. If one acknowledges a desire and then releases it, it prevents the attachment to that craving. As desires arise, release them the same way any thought is released. The Noble Eightfold Path explains that Wisdom, Ethical Conduct, and Concentration free us from the attachments and delusions caused by desire.

Instead of ignoring our desires and pretending that they are not there, we can acknowledge and work with them until we are familiar enough with ourselves and our minds to rise above unnecessary desires. Love and acceptance of ourselves and where we are on our personal journey are powerful tools. Life is a learning process and we want to work lovingly with our cravings until we can overcome them.

Desire is a non-acceptance of the current moment. When we accept what we have and what we do not have, we can be joyful either way. The 14th Dalai Lama said, "When your mind is peaceful, relaxed, and happy, eternal pleasures such as good food, clothing, and conversation make things even better, but their absence does not overpower you." [15]

Freedom from desire allows us to see what pleasure we already have without fixating on what we do not have. Then we can clearly see how full our lives are.

Surrender and Detach

> Man has nothing else to do but surrender—in deep
> trust, in deep love. Don't be a doer, just surrender.
> Let there be a let-go.
> – Osho: Spiritual Teacher and Writer [16]

When we detach from "needing" a specific outcome, we open ourselves up to receiving it. This does not mean we can guarantee receiving of wants through detachment; that is still an attempt to control. We want to ask for our desires or create an intention to get them, and then release the *need* to have them. This allows us to understand our desires and then release them.

Whether you believe in a Higher Power or not, you can still

release your "needs." Needing something does not make us more likely to receive it. Instead, we can acknowledge what we want, work toward it if we decide to, and let go of the fear of not having it. This is a useful form of desire and passion.

The happier we become with Right Now, the less we have desires. All desires stem from a sense of discontent with the current moment: we want what we do not have. The more we live as our true-selves, the less desire we have for situations to be different. When the ego stops attaching to specific ideas, people, places, and things, we relieve the conditions that make our desires necessary, so they disappear on their own.

Surrender to the current moment. We cannot change what *is*. Work toward heart desires with diligence and effortless mastery. There is no force when we live from the heart.

Remember that our heart's desires are always possible. There is a little voice in our heads that tells us that we are unable to achieve them because we are scared. This voice is the very source of much of our insanity! It is a voice that talks us out of what our hearts know to be true, because we are afraid of what we might be capable of if we were unrestricted. Start to hear your heart-desires and abandon the ego-desires. The entire Universe conspires to help us when we act from the heart.

Practice!

1. Observe how often you use the word "need" when you mean "want."

2. Make a quick list of wants and needs. Next to the wants, list why you want them. Is it an ego-desire or a heart-desire? Are your wants worth redirecting your entire life path to achieve them? If you have any needs, go satisfy them.
3. Make a list of your desired goals in life. If any of these goals are incompatible with the others, cross one of them out. Your heart-desires will not conflict, so listen to your inner-self and decide how to proceed.
4. Make a list of intentions, voice them out loud, and then burn the paper. Release your attachment to the outcome. Accept the uncertainty and surrender to the moment. Know that all possibilities are perfect, whether you achieve them or not.
5. If you know your purpose, do not give up on it. Ever. When you live your purpose, your desires disappear naturally because you are fulfilled.
6. **Questions:**

    What is desire?

    Is there a difference between goals and desires?

    Is it wrong or selfish to satisfy desires?

6. IGNORANCE

> The mind is its own place, and in itself can
> make a Heaven of Hell, a Hell of Heaven.
> – John Milton: Poet and Writer [1]

A Sufi parable describes five men who have never seen an elephant before. They stand in a pitch black room and one by one they touch the creature in an attempt to understand it. The first man feels the trunk and describes the elephant as a water-pipe creature. The second touches only the ear and describes it as a fan. The third feels the leg and thinks it is a column. The fourth man runs his hands on the ridges of the back and knows it to be a throne. The last touches the tusk and declares it is made of porcelain.[2] All of these men experienced the elephant for themselves and believed, without a shadow of a doubt, that their perceptions were "right."

Our perceptions are skewed by ignorance and misunderstanding. We perceive life incorrectly and then swear by the false facts. We base incorrect conclusions off of false information and our entire worldview becomes convoluted. Our perception of the Elephant is incomplete, yet we believe that we know and understand it all, because of what we have personally experienced.

Ignorance is the state of being uneducated, unaware, and uninformed. When we live in ignorance, we unknowingly and unconsciously make decisions that hurt ourselves and others. For example, disinformation campaigns were used in both the Cold War and World War II for political control, military tactics, and manipulation. In another example, advertising relies on false promises and illusions to convince us to buy products we do not need. Both of these reveal that what we do not know *can* hurt us.

Ignorance is caused by attachment to fallacy. When we attach to a specific idea, real or not, we disregard truth and logic, because we need the belief to be real. Sometimes we even become so attached to specific ideas or results that we delude ourselves into believing what we know to be inaccurate; we do not take the time to perceive a situation to its full extent; we just find proof that our worldview is correct and then we stop looking.

Ignorance perpetuates suffering, but the information itself is not the culprit. Information is neutral; it is the choices we make using the information that lead to either suffering or happiness.

There is no doubt that Truth *exists* (i.e., how things *are*) but we are unable to view or understand it because of misperceptions, attachments, and delusions that get in the way. Without realizing, we attach feeling and meaning to our experiences and create beliefs accordingly; we unquestioningly assume that our perceptions are accurate and unbiased.

Awareness of self allows us to experience life as it *exists*. We cannot win a chess game if we do not understand the rules or watch our opponent's actions. Through conscious effort and attention, we can eliminate the distortions in our reality and be free of delusions.

Senses of Perception

> Up to the Twentieth Century, reality was everything humans could touch, smell, see, and hear. Since the initial publication of the chart of the electromagnetic spectrum, humans have learned that what they can touch, smell, see, and hear is less than one-millionth of reality.
> – Buckminster Fuller: Philosopher and Inventor [3]

We fixate on the physical world around us and assume that it is the *only thing going on around us*. We assume that there could be no other factors besides the ones we experience, but we understand the Universe about as much as a cockroach understands our world. We do not have the senses to even perceive some things, (e.g., infrared, ultraviolet, echolocation, electrical fields, night vision, etc.) nor the mental capacity to process others. We see a very small portion of *existence*, and we understand even less.

Even the miniscule amount of Reality that we do recognize is mostly made up. The brain processes and analyzes our physical perceptions and links them together in strings of thought. The mind fills in the gaps of our physical perceptions so seamlessly that we do not realize that our five senses are compilations of electrical signals:

Sight: Sight takes place mostly in the brain and is subject to interpretation by it. A complex system of lens to retina to neurons calculates and compiles what comes out as "vision." What we see is not what is there though. The lens projects the world upside down and our depth perception is compiled from visual clues. There are also blind spots in our vision (try the Blind Spot Test) and optical illusions that "move" and "morph." All of these show that what we see is not necessarily what is there.

Touch: The body sometimes misdirects pain and pleasure to other parts, phantom limbs register appendages that are not there, and children do not cry until they see an injury or we react to it. Some people laugh when tickled, while some despise it, both of which are emotional ties to physical sensations.

Sound: Our ears "mishear" words that people say and sometimes we fill in sounds that are not there. "Did you hear that?"

Taste: Some love spicy food and some love sweets; some love veggies and some love meats. While a lot of our taste may be genetic, there is a huge mental-emotional tie to the food we eat. Perhaps you hate the taste of broccoli because it reminds you of daycare or you like apple pie the way Mom used to make it.

Smell: Our olfactory senses are in the same area of the brain as memory and feelings. Perhaps tobacco reminds you of Grandpa or juniper reminds you of the old ranch.

Our minds influence the situations we "experience." Have you ever seen a black jacket out of the corner of your eye and thought it was your black dog? Or perhaps you distinctly remember grabbing your phone, but then you do not have it. All perceptions are neural flashes in the brain and the mind makes interpretations about them. It is not uncommon for children to be afraid of the dark because the shadows look like monsters. To the child, the shadows *are* monsters. Our brains fill in the misunderstandings from our perceptions.

We want to believe that our worldview is only based on "facts," but with our limited perception of the world, we do not experience enough to make that claim. We see a small portion of the Elephant, yet we think we understand the whole Elephant.

The physical world seems so real to us that it can be difficult to understand that it is a mental construct. Our sight, sound, smell, taste, and touch are just information until our minds interpret it. Our "experience" of the world is determined by how our brain analyzes the information that we take in with our five senses and most of this is lightning fast.

As incredible as it seems, most of our world is imagined from within the mind. The world we experience is made up. The question is: who is making it up?

Beyond Belief

> Living is easy with eyes closed,
> misunderstanding all you see.
> – The Beatles: Music Group [4]

The ego is a great ignorance propagator. It relies on tricking us into believing false stories and remembering situations incorrectly to convince us of its agenda. We unknowingly fall into many illusions to satisfy the ego:

Beliefs

Our beliefs impact our perceptions of the world. We understand the idiom, "Seeing is believing," but it also goes the other way: believing is seeing. When we have a belief or idea, our brains create it in our "reality;" our vision is constructed according to our mind's eye. Everything we see we construct with our minds first; this includes color, shading, texture, motion, shape, visual objects, depth perception, and entire visual scenes. [5] The eyes create visually what is first invented in our minds.

Our brains also filter out information that does not apply to our worldview, while highlighting the information that does. We believe an idea or concept and then we see it. "Whatever the Thinker thinks, the Prover proves." [6] This means that whatever we think, our mind will seek to prove. We believe an idea to be true, and so it is… at least to us. We create a kind of tunnel vision—a reality tunnel—for ourselves. Once we decide on a belief, our minds shut down all other possibilities. [7]

Our outside experiences mirror our inside experiences. Our physical perceptions of the world are impacted by the constant streaming inner monologue of our minds. We think that "something bad happened," so "I am unhappy," but actually we were unhappy, so we found an external source to pinpoint the emotion onto. Sometimes we go searching at great lengths to find an external "reason" for our internal suffering. Then we make up elaborate lies and believe them in order to maintain that level of suffering.

Once we believe an idea, we attach to it and our egos make sure we never see any evidence to the alternative. If we decide a concept is true, and it is not, then we seek to prove the fallacy to ourselves over and over again. Even if we believe an idea that *is* true, it can still cause us to misperceive a situation or make false assumptions about it. Whatever we believe on the inside will be pushed onto the outside. We perceive what we already think to be true, regardless of whether it is or not.

The ego loves beliefs; they shape our whole existence, way of life, and "who we are." If the ego can convince us to believe an idea, or latch on to an existing belief, it gains immense power over us.

The ego creates and invents beliefs to control us. If a situation happens to discredit one of those belief systems, the ego forces it to be real through lies and misperceptions. If we believe the square block will fit into the circular hole, the ego will hammer it in until it fits. Whenever it does not fit, we make it fit, even if it means a great deal of effort. Sometimes we even reroute our entire lives to make sure our beliefs stay intact.

Misunderstanding

We rarely take the time to experience and understand our surroundings. Much of our ignorance happens because we do not comprehend a situation before we make an assumption about it, we do not approach situations with an open mind, or we prejudge. Expectation of what is going to happen and how it will happen leads us to attach to a specific idea and we are blind to any alternatives. If we instead approach a situation ready to accept anything, we are more likely to perceive it as it truly *exists,* rather than see and experience illusions.

We want to "accept not expect" all that happens. Our minds do not know the difference between what we think happens in a situation and what actually happens. If we let our minds run away with possibilities, we are unable to see the situation with a clean-slate. We have already loaded up our view of reality with fallacy. When we jump to conclusions about how a situation is happening or will happen, our vision is clouded from the Truth.

Falsified Memories

Our memories are not infallible. Once a situation is stored in our memories, we can reinvent and remember it falsely. For example, a child blames their siblings saying, "I didn't do anything!" or "She started it!" It is easy to make slight changes to a situation to make it appear in a different light. When it serves our egos, we just change the facts a bit. Our memories serve our beliefs and egos; we compile our ideas about "how the world works" by misremembering life.

We think that our memories are facts, but we often based the original situation off of false beliefs, misremembered the situation, and then tweaked it to our liking.

Working with Belief

> It does not do to leave a live dragon out of
> your calculations, if you live near him
> – J.R.R. Tolkien: Writer and Professor [8]

Beliefs affect how we think at a very deep level. The mind is the filter between us and our external world and it dictates what we experience. To prevent ignorance, we want to be very careful about the beliefs that we subscribe to, be aware of ourselves, and know how our ideas influence us.

Our brains seek to prove whatever we believe, so we want to make sure that our beliefs bring happiness. There is no reason to hold on to a belief that leads to misery. For example, if someone believes that the world is out to get them, they might unconsciously seek out harmful interactions. In another example, the Law of Attraction is the belief that our thoughts create our reality. One of the requirements for this system to work is the *belief* that it is real; it "works" because we then become ignorant to all situations where it does not work. Even if a belief is true, it can still be used to delude ourselves from other truths. As we work through our beliefs, we can rearrange and remove the ideas that do not serve us.

We may never understand Reality as it *exists,* free of ignorance; there are so many factors filtered into our consciousness that it is probably impossible to find an unbiased version of Reality. However, our chosen beliefs impact us greatly. The world of a scientist is different from the world of a spiritual teacher. Knowing this can literally change our lives.

We do not have to abandon all our beliefs in this process. We just want to be very careful about the beliefs we subscribe to, since they play a large role in our individual realities. Asking questions like, "Why do I have this belief?" "What would life be like without it?" and "Can I abandon this idea?" can be helpful.

Putting our assumed beliefs under scrutiny causes them to either strengthen or be let go. When we allow ourselves to honestly challenge beliefs, we either come up with more validity for them or we find evidence that counters them. Challenging ideas in a healthy way allows us to release the ones that no longer serve us.

Before we can challenge our beliefs, we must first allow ourselves the possibility that our beliefs do not serve us. A strong acceptance and stability of self allows us the strength to challenge beliefs without falling apart. The ego relies on beliefs to define us. We must first have strength in ourselves before we can challenge them.

When we start to release our attachment to ideas, it is not uncommon to experience fear. When we experience fear at the idea of abandoning a belief, we know that the belief is not coming from a place of Love. Fear implies that the belief is attached to the ego-self. The inner-knowledge of the heart never causes fear, even at the absence of an idea. If our hearts know an idea to be true and we attempt to abandon that wisdom, life seems less complete and less fulfilling, but it is not fearful.

The inner knowing of the heart cannot experience fear at the loss of an idea, because it is a state of being. No idea or concept can threaten our state of being. If we come to our beliefs in love and acceptance, we can start allowing ourselves to release beliefs that hinder our life experience.

Challenging our beliefs can be difficult, since many of them are tied into our idea of "self." If your religious and spiritual beliefs serve you, keep them, but I challenge you to not absorb all aspects without deep contemplation. Challenge every part of your religious and spiritual beliefs to see if they hold up. Truth will withstand even the strongest questioning. Challenging beliefs will strengthen faith, rather than destroy it.

It is up to you to decide which beliefs serve you and which ones do not. Some beliefs are as simple as, "Nobody likes me," or "I am fat," while others are complex and relate to views of God, Life, and the Universe. Be careful about your beliefs and make the conscious choice to believe in each one that you keep.

Perspective: Gratitude

> We are all in the gutter, but some
> of us are looking at the stars.
> – Oscar Wilde: Poet and Writer [9]

Our perspective impacts what we perceive. What we choose to focus on alters our perceptions. An optimist finds the positive qualities in any situation, while a pessimist finds the negative. Perceptions are the looking glass; they are what allow us to see. Perspective is the angle we take and how we interpret it. In turn, the angle we take then changes what we see.

Gratitude helps us to focus on what is at present and teaches us to be satisfied with it. Learning to be grateful for what we have brings happiness and shifts our focus to joy and contentment. When we notice what we have, we stop dwelling on what we do not have. This slight perspective shift can change our entire experience of the world.

> Riches are not from abundance of worldly goods, but from a contented mind.
> – Muhammad: Founder of Islam [10]

Embracing gratitude and happiness does not mean that we refuse to see the difficulties. Refusing to accept the struggles in life does not make them go away; they get more difficult when ignored. We want to be grateful for that which brings us pleasure, as well as that which brings suffering. It all exists for a reason, teaching us valuable lessons. Gratitude for all situations and experiences shifts our internal perspective and changes how our physical world appears.

It is easy to accept life when it goes how we want it to; when it does not, we get upset. At this point, we attempt to force the result we want. This attempt to change a situation leads to ignorance of the real one. Acceptance of all situations, without labeling them as "good" or "bad" helps us to avoid attachment to specific ideas about the world.

When we think of one situation as more favorable than another, we attach to that idea. This creates a belief about "How the world should be," that the ego then upholds. If we accept all that happens, we understand the real situations as they occur, and then make decisions based on facts, rather than decisions based on delusions.

There is no way to change what has already occurred. Sometimes, the best we can do is accept that they happened and move on. If we accept a situation as it *is*, rather than trying to alter it, we can find the happiness in any situation. *Gratitude is a choice.*

Love versus Ignorance

> The world was beautiful when looked at in
> this way—without seeking, so simple, so childlike.
> – Hermann Hesse: Nobel Prize in Literature [11]

It is impossible to have ignorance and Real Love in the same place. Real Love comes from an unconditional understanding and acceptance. Ignorance is a lack of understanding.

When we do not understand a situation, we cannot accept it for what it *is,* because we accept our *idea.* That idea is a false image and we are misinformed in our assumptions about it. This makes us ignorant and incapable of true acceptance.

Ignorance of our actual surroundings prevents us from living to our full capacity. We spend a lot of energy trying to force life into the box we decide upon, and then we expend even more energy to correct these false perceptions later on.

We mirror these actions within ourselves as well. We decide that our true-selves are a certain person and then we expend energy to force them into being. Ignorance stops us from loving and accepting ourselves, or anyone else, because we are lost in delusion. Acceptance is a key to Love and ignorance is a barrier in reaching that door.

When we clear our minds of the false information, we are free to view the world as it *exists,* in True Beauty. Take a hike on a cool summer day to a place all by yourself; there is no hate or suffering there. Suffering exists in the world because we create it there. We want to give all of life an open mind and then respond to it in Love.

We can only filter information thoroughly if we carefully consider every piece that comes to us, without bias, and this only happens when we have a clear mind. With consciousness, we can process information using discernment and non-attachment to specific outcomes. To get a clear look of Reality, we must avoid snap judgments and auto-filtering of ideas according to prejudices. Clarity allows us to see the world as it truly *exists*—paradise—rather than the hell we turn it into.

> We see things not as they are, but as we are ourselves.
> – Henry Major Tomlinson: Writer and Journalist [12]

The world is whatever we believe it to be. As we learn to accept ourselves, we learn to accept the world. When we have seen our strongest inner demons and accepted them, the world is no challenge. Overcoming ignorance in ourselves is one of the most difficult steps we can take. Siddhartha Gautama listed ignorance as one of the primary causes of suffering.

Our pretend worlds seem easier to escape into than understanding our hardships. Yet, there is always a part of our minds that understands the truth; deceiving ourselves does not make anything easier; it leads to more unhappiness. In his book *Mission of Art,* the visionary artist, Alex Grey said:

> In order to notice our own worldview, we have to think about the way we think; we have to rise above our habitual thought patterns and notice that they are habits. We have to question who we think we are. This happens only when our worldview is sufficiently challenged, when new visions collide with and unsettle our existing vision of life. If the challenge is great enough, our worldview and sense of self will dissolve and either regress, break down, or transform to a higher deeper vision.[13]

When we allow ourselves to challenge our beliefs, perceptions, and attachments, we free ourselves to see the world as it *is*. We can change our perceptions and perspective of life with conscious effort.

We choose how to view our world. If a situation makes us unhappy, we can pick a different perspective. We select our reality and we can pick one that brings happiness. The moment we choose a different reality tunnel, we tumble down a new rabbit hole and our lives change to prove it to us.

Practice!

1. Make a list of your beliefs: spiritual, physical, emotional, etc. Challenge each on every level. If done thoroughly, this exercise is uncomfortable.

2. Strive to listen and understand people and situations before you make a decision about them. Assume that you do not fully understand what is going on.
3. Drop your "story." Whatever story you have created for yourself to explain your past is false. At this point, the ego has figured out what it wants to say about you and has manipulated your "story" to reflect that.
4. Find things that you are grateful for every day. Gratitude shifts your focus from what you do not have to what you do have; it is contentment with the current moment.
5. Make a list of what makes you unhappy. Find a way to accept each one of these. You can only be unhappy because of your ignorance about the perfection that lies in them.
6. **Questions:**

    What is ignorance?

    What is Reality?

    Is there a difference between belief and faith?

7. COMPASSION

> When your perspective includes the suffering of limitless beings, your own suffering looks comparatively small.
> – Dalai Lama XIV: Spiritual Leader of Tibet [1]

Once upon a time, a man asked to see heaven. He was told that he would have to see hell first. The man agreed. In hell there was a gigantic banquet table containing the most delicious food imaginable. However, the diners had long forks for hands and could not reach their mouths, so they starved. The man was then taken to heaven and saw the exact same situation, but instead of fiendishly stabbing at the food and failing, the people were happily feeding each other. [2]

The more we dwell on ourselves, the less we focus on the feelings and ideas of others. When we focus exclusively on our own issues, we become apathetic and unaware of the pain and suffering of the world. In selfishness, we lose sight of what it means to be compassionate and share this planet.

In the quest to love ourselves, we do not want to forget compassion. Loving ourselves leads to loving the world, but we do not want to ignore others in the process. In fact, learning compassion for others will help us learn love for ourselves.

Our culture tells us that it is "every man for himself," and this idea causes us to ignore the needs of others. Many of us are afraid to "waste" time and energy on someone else, thinking there will not be enough left for us. We fear that we will be trampled by the stampede of people struggling to climb to the top, and then we focus so hard on getting ourselves to the top that we ignore the people we trample along the way. Many of us believe that we do not need help and that everyone should take care of themselves.

The less compassionate we are, the less we realize or care when others need assistance. We view others as our competition and fear helping them. In this type of world, we become more and more isolated in the attempt to be The Best and we become more and more miserable in the process.

Compassion is not new. Many world religions preach compassion. The Golden Rule of "Treat others as you wish to be treated," dates back to Ancient Babylon in 1780 BC. [3]

> **Islam:** Allah is referred to as Rahman, "The Compassionate." [4] Rahman is the most special of the Names of God. Nearly every chapter in the Quran begins with the name of Rahman.
> **Christianity:** The Bible says, "Blessed are the merciful, for they will be shown mercy," [5] and "If someone strikes you on the right cheek, turn to him the other also. And if someone wants to sue you and take your tunic, let him have your cloak as well. …

Give to the one who asks you, and do not turn away from the one who wants to borrow from you." [6]

Judaism: In Hebrew, God is referred to as El Rachum, "The God of Compassion." [7]

Hinduism: Daya (compassion) is a central virtue in both Hinduism and Sikhism. [8] This teaching dates all the way back to the Vedas, which were written sometime before 1500 BC.

Buddhism: Compassion is the antidote to anger and one of the solutions to suffering in general. The 14th Dalai Lama said, "If you want others to be happy practice compassion; and if you want yourself to be happy practice compassion." [9]

The idea that we are "better off alone," is a new idea that causes great misery to many.

Shared Vulnerability

> If we have no peace, it is because we have
> forgotten that we belong to each other.
> – Mother Teresa: Nobel Peace Prize [10]

We develop and strengthen relationships through shared vulnerability. When we share ourselves and connect with each other on a human level, we create bonds that last past lifetimes. Vulnerability helps us understand the weakness in each of us and we cannot help but honor that fragility of life. It is our fragile natures that make life so sacred.

Our shared weaknesses bring us closer together. Action movies show the leading couple going through traumatic situations and then they end up together in the end. This illustrates how experiencing each other's weaknesses allows us to connect and see each other as true living beings. Conversely, when we portray a "perfect" persona on the outside, we seem untouchable, and people cannot understand us. We shut our true-selves down, block them from others, and we end up disconnected and alone. When we hide our flaws, people can only worship us on a pedestal, but they are unable to be real with us.

We pretend we are superhuman: we cover our aging, we pretend not to get sick, and when people ask how we are, we always reply, "Good." We do not want people to see our flaws, so we cover them up. In doing this we close ourselves off to the beautiful connections that can be formed and built between two equal beings.

When we stop connecting with others, we lose touch with what it means to share this planet. When we build ourselves up as *untouchable*, people are afraid to approach and get in *touch* with us. People can only admire a superhuman from afar and we distance ourselves from everyone when we assume that role.

The less we connect to others, the more closed off we become. We then believe that there is a shortage of love and acceptance, because we dam up the free-flow of energy that occurs by connecting with others. In this type of world, we *must* take care of ourselves, ignoring others, or we perish. The less we help each other, the less friendly our world is in response and the more isolated we each feel.

Breaking the Walls of Apathy

> Science may have found a cure for most evils;
> but it has found no remedy for the worst of
> them all—the apathy of human beings.
> – Helen Keller: Writer and Social Activist [11]

It can be difficult to break free from apathy. Oftentimes, we are so unstable with our own emotions, thoughts, and lives that we cannot get outside of ourselves for even a moment to consider others. We build ourselves on shaky ground and we spend all of our time just attempting to stabilize. We fear adding more to our plates because we have already bit off more than we can chew.

Learning to connect with others destroys the walls that we create around ourselves and sets the inner-self free. When we do this, we realize that there is no shortage of love, we had just perceived and created a world where that was the case. Apathy is a self-imposed illusion that we can drop the moment we allow ourselves to open up.

Many of us care about others, but we do not know how to express it. This pent-up self is not our natural state; we are stoic out of habit. We learn uncompassionate behaviors without even realizing it and then repeat them back. This behavior is a pattern and it is remedied as soon as we want to change it. Most of us are not apathetic by choice. It is an unconscious behavior that we learn in a multitude of ways:

Expected Apathy: We are not always free to express our emotions. At work and school we are expected to check our emotional baggage at the door and remain "professional." People expect us to repress our emotions and remain unfeeling. The more we practice this, the more it becomes our natural tendency.

Numbness: Feeling for everyone becomes hard and it is "easier" to shut down all emotions than it is to feel them. We believe that suffering will continue, regardless of how we feel about it, so it is easier to not feel it. This world shows us many methods to remain unfeeling and we seldom experience true vulnerability and intimacy with those around us. We do not learn healthy outlets for our inner-suffering, so we repress it and ignore it.

Desensitization: We experience so much pain through media that we get used to it. It then takes increasing amounts of trauma for us to get the same emotional reaction. Then, in life, when people do not express these extreme amounts of emotion, we do not even understand that they are upset.

Inherited Apathy: When we see others act apathetic, we learn that as the appropriate way to react to situations. Television shows us fake-scenes about fake-people and we get used to their fake-suffering. Likewise, newscasters act apathetic, so we mimic their reaction. Our indifference to our fellow man is a self-perpetuating cycle that we inherit from others.

Disconnectedness: We experience life through a screen: windshield screen, computer screen, television screen, phone screen, etc. We do not have much direct interaction with people.

We experience emotions the same way. We forget how to feel and express emotions unless there is an intermediary there. There is no vulnerability when there is a screen between us. Even if someone cries, we do not connect or experience it with them. We forget that communication is an *exchange*, rather than a one-way street.

It is not that people suffer *and* we do not care, instead people suffer *because* we do not care. When we allow ourselves to feel with others, we are compelled to help, even if it is only a tiny bit. It is only possible to allow people to hurt if we do not care about them and we do not care about them if we feel disconnected from them. The more connected we are, the more we care when people hurt and feel motivated to assist them.

Compassion: The Ego Trump Card

> Our task must be to free ourselves from this prison [the delusion of separateness] by widening our circle of compassion to embrace all living creatures and the whole of nature in its beauty.
> – Albert Einstein: Nobel Prize in Physics [12]

Compassion is the new, old way of interacting with the world. We are apathetic because we are scared. It is difficult to experience emotions in such a large capacity when we live in apathy, but the more we practice, the easier it becomes! Compassion is a matter of retraining old patterns.

Compassion is the end of some of the most powerful tactics of the ego: blame, resentment, non-forgiveness, judgment, and non-acceptance. A corrupted ego has no place for consideration of others. If other people are "wrong" and we are "right," then that makes us stronger than them. Judgment and blame assist us in building up our false sense of self.

No matter why someone attacks us, they are a living being. Destructive patterns are a result of inner-suffering: the human race is hurting and we try to understand our pain by hurting other people. Compassion allows us to realize this and love people regardless. Compassion happens when we release the need to be The Best and allow ourselves to become equals.

Caring about others seems stupid and foolish when we are consumed by our egos. We feel that everyone has the same opportunities, so if someone has more than someone else, they worked harder for it. When we believe the world works like this, we do not feel responsible for the suffering of others and we do not have to take time to feel for them. The complication with this perspective is that, for the most part, extreme amounts of money, power, fame, and beauty are given to us. The situation we are born into dictates our possible futures, even if we work hard for it.

We find ourselves justifying that we "deserve" what we have and those without "do not deserve" it. Though anyone can work hard and gain more, the amount of energy expended and the amount of gain received are not the same. We are not all born in equal standings: slaves in the diamond mines of Sierra Leone work all day every day and see no money in return; [13] compare that to a baby millionaire, who earns approximately $107 a day in interest without any effort. As much as we want to believe that we deserve what we have, most of life is "luck of the draw."

The idea that "good things happen to good people and bad things happen to bad people" is an ego-illusion. These statements justify apathy for people who suffer. There is no need to feel for or help others if they are capable of helping themselves. It is an excuse to avoid our responsibility to our fellow man. Rather than take a moment to feel compassion for a person, we justify that they are in their situation because of their own shortcomings.

The ego fixates on how great life would be if we had more and it ignores everyone else. When we take a moment to understand those that are less fortunate than ourselves, we feel guilt and self-hate. Then we shut down our compassion and live as a hungry zombie that must always consume more in order to distract itself.

When we see ourselves as equals, we connect with and understand the suffering of others, knowing we could easily be in their position. When we are all equal, we all deserve "life, liberty, and the pursuit of happiness." [14] If we have more than someone else, we would rather give some to them to assure their happiness than keep it for ourselves, because we realize that we could have been in the same situation.

With compassion, there is no way to justify that our *wants* are more important than anyone else's *needs*. Each creature is a living, breathing, being. It is difficult to explain how a $200,000 car is more important than feeding hungry people, if we are all equal. These games deceive us when we try to become The Best. When we abandon desires of the ego, we want everyone to be happy, rather than just ourselves.

Living in compassion, it is the state of the planet as a whole that impacts us the most. This means that if we decide to skip a meal to feed someone who is starving, we are happier because that person is happy. With compassion, even if we have less, we have more. We are connected to everyone else and we experience the joy of everyone around us. When people hear this, they often remark, "Well if I take less and nobody else does, then I will have less and everyone else will keep taking. It will not change anything." This is not true. When we help someone, we change their life. When we change peoples' lives, we form a bond with them that makes us both stronger. The idea that "we will be less" or "not have enough," is a shallow ego idea that does not make any sense.

Compassion disintegrates the corrupt ego because it takes the focus off of us and puts it on others. The false-self lives solely within us; if we focus on someone else, there is not enough attention on the self to maintain the illusion.

The misguided ego resents others for their happiness because we are not as happy as they are. If we instead connect with others, each victory of someone else is a victory for us as well. We are able to share in the collective happiness of those around us, and therefore we do not constantly require more in order to be happy. In fact, sacrifice brings more joy than receiving ever can, especially when we provide for others in need. We do not all have to be Mother Teresa to understand that compassion and giving bring happiness, while apathy and selfishness do not.

Compassion drives us to naturally help others when we can, and know when to accept the help of others when we need it. This is a loving flow that occurs when we feel and experience the world with other people. Gandhi said:

> Service can have no meaning unless one takes pleasure in it. When it is done for show or for fear of public opinion, it stunts the man and crushes his spirit. Service which is rendered without joy helps neither the servant nor the served. But all other pleasures and possessions pale into nothingness before service which is rendered in a spirit of joy. [15]

Compassion does not mean that we force ourselves to help others. When someone gives because they feel like they have to, it is almost the same as withholding it. Giving in this way creates obligation and debt that must be repaid by the recipient, whether we voice this demand or not. Forced giving and compassion lead to a state of resentment, while giving done out of a desire to share and serve bring us extreme joy.

We do not need to make ourselves *do* anything, just shift our perspectives to others whenever possible. We do not want to forget ourselves, but we want to attempt to understand other people and what they experience. We want to accept and understand what others are going through without dwelling in their emotions. Connecting with people, helping them when we are able, and avoiding taking on their personal suffering helps us find a balance between ourselves and the world.

Learning to feel for other people also equips us to handle our own suffering. The 14th Dalai Lama said:

> It makes practical sense for you, just one being, to opt for taking care of many, but also, by concentrating on the welfare of others, you yourself will be happier. Compassion diminishes fright about your own pain and increases inner strength. It gives you a sense of empowerment, of being able to accomplish your tasks. [16]

When we can look at the broad range of suffering in the world, our own pain seems relatively small and is easy to overcome. We also learn from others and can view our own lives with a broader range of experience.

Whether we connect with people's happiness or their traumas, compassion allows us to understand someone else for a moment, and this opens us up to the world around us. Instead of isolating ourselves within, we attract people to us. Solving a maze is easy when we can see the whole picture, but when we jump inside, it can take hours to solve a very basic puzzle. If we only dwell on our own issues, we do not understand life in all its complexities. When we allow ourselves to see life from someone else's point-of-view, we enrich our knowledge and understanding of how the world truly *is*.

We hate what we do not understand; understanding others weakens the selfish aspects of the ego and releases us to *live in Love*.

Our shared vulnerability allows our true-selves to connect and form unbreakable bonds.

Unity versus Isolation

> All for one, one for all.
> – Alexandre Dumas: Writer [17]

We cannot survive on love alone, but those who love are taken care of by those who love them. It is easier to live in a world where we take care of each other than it is to live in a world where we *must* take care of ourselves. We can survive at a banquet table with gigantic forks for hands if we feed each other. If we only serve ourselves, we all starve.

A compassionate world starts with each of us. When we love and accept others, they learn to be the same way toward us, and our lives change in the process. "It only takes a spark to get a fire going." Be the ember of Love that sparks a fire of compassion in your family and community.

Disconnection and non-acceptance of ourselves has caused us to forget how to connect and accept others. We seldom walk a mile in someone's shoes, unless we plan to steal their shoes. Compassion toward ourselves and those around us opens us up to a world of possibilities and happiness.

Love and acceptance of self lead to a strong desire to help the world. When we love and accept ourselves, we learn how to love and accept others. As we release the ego-self, we become more compassionate and caring. Self-love causes us to be a sturdy post buried deep in the sand and others can lean on us without any danger of our collapse. Stabilizing ourselves frees us to assist others. Once we find Love within, we seek to spread it without.

We love others to the level that we love ourselves, and the more we love and understand ourselves, the freer and more likely we are to feel compassion toward others. Oftentimes, we do not connect with the world because we are afraid to reveal our true-selves, we view independence as a glistening ideal that we strive to become, and the ego thinks that we must always act alone and it is afraid to rely on anybody else. Once we eliminate our self-centered thoughts, it is easy to consider the thoughts and feelings of others.

> No man is an island, entire of itself; every man is a
> piece of the continent, a part of the main.
> – John Donne: Poet [18]

No matter how hard we strive to detach from everyone else, none of us are alone; isolation is not real. We rely on money, economy, jobs, and culture to provide for us. We are all connected to each other and we cannot separate from anyone. The Six Degrees of Kevin Bacon was a popular trivia game in the '90s that illustrated what a small world we live in. This game teaches us that it is possible to link many people within six steps.

Independence is an illusion that makes us feel strong and powerful. When we realize how connected we all are, we want to help others. If we trick ourselves into believing we are isolated, it is easy to feel apathetic. An unhealthy ego likes the idea of isolation because it means it can serve itself and that it does not have to care for others.

The ego requires isolation and independence to make up for the fact that it feels weak and powerless. It strives to become better than others and puts people down in order to build itself up. When we love and accept ourselves as we truly *exist*, the ego has no need to play these games. We can abandon the need for isolation, because we know that we are strong in ourselves.

Compassion makes the world a friendly place and it strengthens everyone: we share experiences, love, vulnerability, intimacy, help each other, unify, and become more fulfilled. On the opposite side, when we are selfish, each of us feels apathetic, empty, lost, and helpless. Without compassion, we live in a world that could care less about us and we could care less about it.

As human beings, we hate seeing people suffer, and hate ourselves over letting them suffer. The pain of others reminds us of the darkness in ourselves. We survive this suffering in a state of delusional apathy by distracting ourselves and filling our lives with mindless distractions. Then we justify apathy saying, "That is how the world is." We like to help each other, but when we get wrapped up in our ego's desire to be The Best, we resist assisting each other.

We inevitably have times of judgment and blame, but this gives us the opportunity for compassion and a chance to overcome these harmful feelings. When we do slip up and judge people, we can learn to forgive and release. The ego gets ideas of revenge when someone harms us and it is easy to listen to these thoughts rather than try to understand the other person and why they hurt us. We believe that it is easier to hate people for their actions than it is to let the feelings go. Compassion leads to a stronger sense of happiness and fulfillment in everyone.

The only thing between us and a more compassionate world is the desire to become more compassionate. We are presented with a dozen ways a day to help us practice. From there, it is a matter of creating new habits.

Compassion understands and accepts others as they are and releases our judgments; it means we cannot blame people for their own shortcomings. When we experience compassion, we cannot attack people, instead, we learn to accept and forgive them. A corrupt ego does not like this, because it loses its ability to blame and hate others.

We can start by treating ourselves with love and compassion, and then love our neighbors as ourselves. Learning compassion, forgiveness, and acceptance for all life transforms the world.

Compassion takes many forms: finance, emotional support, volunteering, kindness, forgiveness, etc. Sometimes we find ourselves thinking that we do not have enough to give, but more often than not, people just want us to *listen* and understand them, and not just wait for our chance to speak. Making the world a more compassionate place is easy. We can start by being with and forgiving each other.

Vulnerability gives us the chance to connect with each other. When we accept our own flaws and vulnerabilities, we are capable of sharing them with others.

We experience compassion to the level that we experience

compassion for ourselves. When we open up, we see the True Beauty that *exists*.

Practice!

1. Listen to people. Let yourself feel each word they tell you and understand why they feel the way they do. Ask questions.
2. Get in the habit of giving. Give slightly more than you are comfortable: leave a large tip, donate to charity, take a friend to lunch, give your leftovers away, or listen to a friend. Find acts of giving and service that you can add into your life.
3. Practice compassion when watching movies, the news, television, etc. Feel what is happening, even if the people are fictional. Is it entertaining to watch people suffer when you feel compassion? Can you sit by and do nothing?
4. Kindness is contagious. It spreads extremely fast and before you know, it takes over your life. Let it infect every aspect of your existence.
5. **Questions:**
   What is compassion and what does it look/feel like?
   Is it wrong to be selfish?
   Is there a difference between isolation of the self and solitude?

8. ANGER

> Fear is the path to the dark side. Fear leads to anger.
> Anger leads to hate. Hate leads to suffering.
> – Yoda: *Star Wars* [1]

Anger is a quick way to make people afraid of us and fear is its own source of power. In the ego's desire to become "better," we resort to aggression, bullying, threatening, revenge, and other fear tactics to manipulate others. We are rewarded when we get angry and people give us what we want, so we seldom look within ourselves to understand how and why it happens. It seems easier to blame others for our anger than it is to figure out why we have it in the first place.

Contrary to popular belief, no one can make us angry. The ego targets outside sources for emotions, but they start inside of us. Anger externalizes internal issues so that we do not have to look inside of ourselves.

We trap pain and fear within and then need a way to resolve

them. Anger is a secondary emotion that provides the release of these internal emotional states: [2]

> **Pain:** Anger is a tool to repress suffering. When we run away from our internal torment, the ego hides it beneath anger. We do not want to discover the wounds within, so we get mad. This covers up the pain, but it does not resolve the initial cause for it and the sore still festers inside of us. When we fully experience emotions, they dissipate and clear away. If we can trace anger back to the original pain that caused it, it diffuses.
>
> **Fear:** Anger can come from a place of fear and has the same physical reactions. Rage is an almost automatic reaction to fear, because we require the increase in strength to conquer our opponent. In a battle, it may be our anger that empowers us to win, but sometimes we produce adrenaline and there is no fight to be fought. When the body prepares for fight or flight and nothing happens, it creates inner tension, anxiety, and angst. Anger then steps in to help us relieve this frustration.

Self-Anger

> What others think of us would be of little
> moment did it not, when known, so deeply
> tinge what we think of ourselves.
> – George Santayana: Poet and Writer [3]

Anger is self-perpetuated; we create suffering through non-acceptance of ourselves and the world, and then we hate and blame external sources for our internal chaos. Anger rejects a situation and seeks to relieve its dissatisfaction through physical force. This is the attempt to deny reality and change it. Anger is a powerful way to avoid accepting the world, while forcing our ideals.

Self-anger is caused by non-acceptance of our true-selves. When we hate or betray our inner-selves, we develop anger to run away from the suffering. We can target other people for these feelings, but taking responsibility for our internal state is the way to heal it. People can attempt to hurt us, but we decide how to feel about it.

Self-hate and acting contrary to our true-selves causes frustration and anger in the attempts to cover the obscene amounts of pain. Frustration and disrespect are the main external sources that set off the ego. [4] We believe that these external sources "cause" us to be angry, but both of these stimuli start with self-hate and self-betrayal:

> **Frustration:** Frustration happens when we expect a result that does not occur. We had an idea or result in mind, and when it was not fulfilled, we became upset. When ego-desires are not fulfilled, we feel worthless and weak because the ego-façade crumbles. We then blame external sources for this internal emptiness.
>
> **Disrespect:** If we can make someone afraid of us, we can control them and then we can assert our power over them. Anger is a way to gain power. When we perceive condescension or weakness of self, the ego retaliates in a power play.

The more confidence and acceptance we have in ourselves and our own paths, the less possible it is for someone to disrespect or frustrate us. No one can disrespect us unless we accept that they have; it requires our own agreement with them. Loving ourselves eliminates this as a possibility. When we respect ourselves, it does not matter how people treat us, because what other people think is none of our business and we do not require validation of others. Likewise, when we accept life as it *is*, we cannot become frustrated, because we do not expect a different result.

Both disrespect and frustration fall away when we accept ourselves. Gandhi purposefully rode in third-class, dealing with immense hardship, and considered it to be a service to mankind, because he was not putting himself above others. [5] With love and acceptance, anger becomes non-existent.

The Anger Voice

> He is not strong and powerful who throweth people down; but he is strong who witholdeth himself from anger.
> – Muhammad: Founder of Islam [6]

Anger can be destructive, but there is nothing "wrong" with it. It is a method that our egos came up with to handle our inner suffering, tension, fear, and repression. The issue with anger is that it causes us to act ways that we do not want to. We find ourselves yelling some pretty harsh statements in the "heat of the moment," and later regretting the damage we inflicted on someone else.

When we let anger get a hold of us, we lose conscious awareness of ourselves and put the ego in power. Anger is one of the ego's greatest tools because it gives it free-reign over us. Our misguided egos are very talented at hijacking, using, and abusing our body's natural anger response. Sometimes they even attach labels to us about our anger and connect it to our "identity." When we say destructive affirmations like, "I have a quick temper," or "I like a good fight," we attach anger to our "personality," which is then maintained by the ego.

Our egos hold on to anger long after the original pain has passed because they like having it as a tool to control us. We harbor feelings of resentment, blame, and judgment as a way to stay angry at others; this is a game the misguided ego uses to keep anger as an option for manipulation.

We can overcome anger when we realize that it is just a habitual ego voice. Our synapses fire in specific pathways, and the more we enforce them, the easier that pathway becomes. We are what we practice. When we practice love and acceptance, they become our initial response.

Consciousness of anger allows us to separate ourselves from it. We do not have to do what the Anger Voice tells us to do. Our anger is not us and we can listen to it in an unbiased perspective, choosing to act only when its ideas are constructive.

Applying Anger

> Your anger is a gift!
> – Rage Against the Machine: Music Group [7]

Even when we realize that we are irate, we become irrational and unable to stop ourselves. It feels intense to be mad and we are so tempted by the power attained by anger that we have a hard time denying ourselves that pleasure.

There is no use hating ourselves over anger. It is a natural process that is in place for our survival. Hating ourselves over an age-old reaction is ineffective.

We use anger to release inner tension, and for some of us, this is the only way we ever release it. Imagine yourself as a teapot on a stove. The more heat we add (repression), the more desperately our true-selves strive to get out. Sometimes this means a forceful whistle as our inner-selves struggle to get free. The more we let our true-selves out, the less pressure builds up.

We want to avoid anger when possible and work with it in healthy ways when it is not. Anger can be helpful; it is a signal as to what is amiss inside of us. Whenever we get angry, we can use it as a clue into ourselves and what we do not accept.

It is very possible for the Anger Voice to give us useful advice. Perhaps it tells us to stay away from certain people or encourages us to take action and change. If your job makes you angry and upset, then the Anger Voice might tell you to quit and get a new job. When we listen to our anger without attaching to it, we can take its input and determine how to respond. In this example, it might mean taking steps toward finding a new job. If we listen to the Anger Voice without bias, we can take actions to remedy the situation in a method that brings happiness.

It is often anger that puts the "rage" in "encourage." It can give us the wake up call that we need to make large and difficult changes. Our anger can serve us well, when we listen to it without attaching to it. The 14th Dalai Lama said:

> 'Anger,' as it is understood in English, can be positive in very special circumstances. These occur when anger is motivated by compassion or when it acts as an impetus or a catalyst for a positive action. In such rare circumstances anger can be a positive whereas hatred can never be positive. [8]

There is a cause for every emotion. They reveal what is happening within and we can use them to grow and learn. Instead of becoming frustrated with anger, we can understand that it is a way to force out the feelings we bottle inside; it shows us how we have betrayed our true-selves.

As we learn to understand and accept ourselves, sometimes we still react in anger. Eventually we can learn to overcome this, but we want to find healthy ways to redirect and release our anger when we cannot.

The intense energy that comes with anger contains great potential, but we use it in destructive ways that hurt each other. We use rage to tear down, rather than to build up. Anger causes wars, battles, and fights which result in mass destruction and death. On the other hand, anger can be used to create music, poetry, dance, and change. When we learn to direct the energy that comes with anger in constructive ways, we can create beauty, instead of destroying it.

> The Buddha compared holding onto anger to grasping
> a hot coal with the intent of throwing it at someone
> else. You, of course, are the one who gets burned.
> – Joan Borysenko: Physician and Writer [9]

Anger is a tempting state, but in the end, it hurts us. However, sometimes we just cannot help ourselves and we pick up the hot coal anyway, knowing full well that it is harmful to ourselves and others. When this happens, we want to drop the coal before we hurt someone with it. This is the equivalent of taking a few moments to count to ten or go for a walk, and then forgiving whatever offense resulted in our anger. Letting go of the coal once we realize that we have grasped it is the way to rise above anger. It is not "bad" to feel mad; we just want to let it go when this happens. The Bible says in Colossians:

> But now you must rid yourselves of all such things as these: anger, rage, malice, slander, and filthy language from your lips ... clothe yourselves with compassion, kindness, humility, gentleness and patience. Bear with each other and forgive whatever grievances you may have against one another. [10]

It can be difficult to release such powerful sensations that anger brings, so finding an outlet to redirect the anger into may be useful. Ideally, we would not pick up the coal at all, but anger can be used as a tool to assist us in our journey when we do.

Conscious Anger

> Any one can get angry—that is easy…but to do
> this to the right person, to the right extent, at the right
> time, with the right motive, and in the right way,
> that is not for everyone, nor is it easy.
> – Aristotle: Philosopher and Scientist [11]

Overcoming anger takes practice. There are a few steps that help us become conscious once our egos have gone crazy with angry passion:

1. **Accept the anger.** When we admit to ourselves that we are angry, we know we are not in a sober state of mind. Increased consciousness helps us identify when we have become unsettled.
2. **Admit that we are irrational.** We cannot trust our thoughts when we are angry, because the ego is calling the shots. Decisions made while angry are not constructive.
3. **Remove ourselves from the situation.** This allows us to stop and regain conscious awareness over our excited minds. Save the discussions and decisions for a later time.
4. **Release the inner tension.** Count to ten, exercise, scream privately, punch a pillow, or create (painting, music, dance, poetry). All of these can provide catharsis for anger.
5. **Forgive ourselves for becoming angry.** Recognize what led to anger and release it. If we resent ourselves for becoming upset, then we perpetuate the feelings that led to anger in the

first place: self-hate and self-betrayal. Instead, we can understand why we became upset and consider what to do in the future to prevent the same situation.

6. **Move on.** Once we forgive ourselves, we can consider how to proceed. If we hurt someone, we can apologize. If we need to finish a discussion, we can have it once we are conscious again. Do not rush this last step, it can take time before we are prepared to move on and fully forgive.

Learning to accept our true-selves and embracing fear dissolves anger naturally, but this is a process that takes time. Always be patient. Anger is strong, but its passion is quick and fleeting. It is a vicious storm, but we can hunker down and wait it out. According to Thich Nhat Hahn, we can address the Anger Voice directly:

> The first function of mindfulness is to recognize, not to fight. 'Breathing in, I know that anger has manifested in me. Hello, my little anger.' And breathing out, 'I will take good care of you.' [12]

Naming aspects of the ego allows us to listen, understand, and release.

Anger forces us to direct our creative energy in the way that *it chooses*. When we rise above it, our passionate energy can be directed how *we choose*. Healing ourselves of anger will not take away our passion; it is the opposite. We feel anger when we do not accurately express ourselves. As we heal, our passion comes out as joy, enthusiasm, and excitement, rather than anger and rage.

We can conquer our anger by mastering our fears and stopping our self-abuse. Through love and acceptance, the catalysts for anger fall away until we drop them entirely. We free ourselves to think more clearly, even in the most trepidatious of situations. By raising our awareness of our own thoughts and actions, we can learn to hear the anger in our heads before we act on it.

Our anger is a clue into our psyche and our true feelings. Once we can view our anger without attaching to it, we can redirect the passion and energy attained from it in ways that are helpful to us. As we heal ourselves, anger disappears.

Practice!

1. What makes you angry? How is the situation caused by fear or pain? Search deep!
2. Find healthy ways to express anger.
3. Practice makes perfect. Anger is difficult to master. Be patient and forgiving as you develop new habits.
4. **Questions:**
   What is anger?
   Who benefits from anger?
   How does anger affect our state of being?

9. CONSCIOUSNESS

> When each day is the same as the next, it's because
> people fail to recognize the good things that happen
> in their lives every day that the sun rises.
> – Paulo Coelho: Poet and Writer [1]

Consciousness is the awareness of one's own existence, sensations, thoughts, and surroundings. Descartes famous quote, "I think therefore I am," explains that if there is an "I" to do the thinking, a being must exist to think it. This "I" is considered to be our presence, however, awareness of self and consciousness occur when we are aware of what is going on within us. Consciousness is a state of experiencing ourselves as we *exist*, in the current moment.

We assume that because we are capable of being conscious, it automatically makes us conscious all the time. We think that because we *can* contemplate existence that we are conscious beings. We are very capable of awareness and presence, but consciousness is more than just the *potential* to be aware. When we choose to live unconsciously, reacting to the whims of our minds, we do not act in consciousness.

True presence is hearing the mind, while not being a slave to its perceptions and ideas. This presence in thought is the ability to make decisions with the awareness of ourselves, rather than living on instinct. We all want to think that we are conscious beings, and we all get moments of illumination when we are, but for many of us, these moments are rare. Our time is spent in a somnambulist state, where we are neither awake nor asleep, going through the repetitions and patterns of day-to-day life.

Merely being aware that we are alive is not true consciousness. Most creatures have the perception of being alive in some form and have the desire to stay alive; even the smallest house fly has an instinct to live. We are different from the house fly because of the ability to transcend our instincts. As human beings, we have the option to choose our actions. We can make the decision *not* to act the way our minds tell us to. This is different from most life-forms.

We have to be aware of our thoughts before we can rise above them. The moments when we transcend our instincts and egos, we act in true consciousness because we are aware of our thoughts.

Consciousness means that we can act in ways that bring happiness, rather than out of need. The less healthy our relationships to the ego are, the more they control us without our realizing. The healthier our relationships become, the easier it is to listen without attaching. Awareness and mindfulness free us to experience our inner-selves.

Presence in the Present

> Consciousness is the potential for all creation.
> The more consciousness you have the more
> potential you have to create.
> – Deepak Chopra: Physician and Spiritual Teacher [2]

The key to consciousness is living in the present. Many of us spend so much mental energy dwelling on past events or predicting future ones that we are lost in those ideas. We cannot silence our minds, because we wander in a multitude of thoughts.

When our consciousness drifts to other places and times, we turn over our awareness of this moment to the ego. Then, it makes decisions about what *it* thinks should happen, while we are stuck in unconscious thoughts and unable to stop it. When we shift our focus back to the present, we are mindful of our thoughts as they occur. This moves us out of our ego and into the true-self, which is always present Now.

The past and future are both very tempting mind-states and we get distracted by them for long periods of time, but they are not real. The only moment of creation is the current moment. We cannot time-travel to the past or future to make changes; Now is the only time we can actively use to take action.

The Past

Think only of the past as its
remembrance gives you pleasure.
– Jane Austen: Writer [3]

The past only exists in our minds. Perhaps it was real at some time, but it does not exist in the current moment. Even if we record it, there is no way to verify that the written records are accurate and unbiased. "History is written by the victors." [4]

Without realizing, we change past events in order to make them fit the ego's needs. Our perspectives influence what we think happened in a situation. There are at least two sides of a story though, and it is not uncommon for two people to remember a situation differently. There is no perfect way to guarantee the past happened a specific way, whether it was our personal past or historical, yet we get hung up on it and let it create suffering in our current moment.

Our memories are not flawless: we forget or amplify certain aspects and the ego alters situations. At the point when thoughts become memories, they cease to exist in any real form. If we get stuck in the past, we are stuck in a fantasy.

There is nothing "real" about the past as it exists in the present. We remember "the good old days," or when "things were better;" these enhance the past and make it more desirable than the current moment. Other times, we demean the past with elaborate stories, "He was so mean to me," or "My childhood was so awful;" we dwell on painful memories or hold grudges and these bring unhappiness to the current moment by dwelling in our suffering. Neither of these mind-states leads to joy, because they distract from Right Now, which is where Reality *is*.

There is no harm in remembering the past, but dwelling in memories wastes the current moment and sacrifices it to an idea that does not exist. If we view our memories with consciousness, we can re-experience the memory as it drifts into our minds, know that it is not Reality, and then consciously let it go. In this way, the past can bring a smile as we remember what brought us here, without losing ourselves.

The Future

> I never think of the future, it comes soon enough.
> – Albert Einstein: Nobel Prize in Physics [5]

We fear and hope for life to be a certain way and base our actions Now off of how they will affect us later, but the future is a projection. We can watch the great movies the ego designs for us, but that does not make them real.

Educated guesses and actions in the present moment lead us in a certain direction, but there is no way to guarantee the results. If we attach to certain results and have an expectation for the world, then we can become angry or upset when they do not turn out that way. Future-dwelling causes us to spend a lot of time wishing for illusions and denying how Reality *is*.

When we future-live, we spend our time thinking of how life will be *someday*. Either Right Now is "not good enough" or we fear it will change. Regardless, we do not enjoy what we already have and we take our sites off of the present.

When we focus on the future, we make that a habit. This means that even if we achieved the future we were looking toward, we would not realize it, because we have the habit of waiting and looking to the future for a better day.

All change happens in the present. If our hearts have a desire, we can make changes Today to move toward it. However, if we sacrifice the present moment in order to make the future "better," we sacrifice the one thing we truly have. This habit takes us away from the present and we are likely to spend the rest of our lives sacrificing Now for a life that may never come.

We do not want to fixate on the future, but goals can serve us well. Focus can encourage us to spread happiness and love. The most important part is to make sure our ambitions bring joy Right Now, as well as later.

We do not want our goals to be the attempts of our egos to attain grandeur. It is easy to make goals "to become better." This is another way to admit to ourselves that we are "not good enough." It is a sneaky way for the ego to tell us we are worthless and fixate on the future when we will be "better." This gives the ego power to dictate our actions in the present. We want to make sure that any goals we set are not a way to serve our egos.

Hard work is fulfilling, but at some point it can become exhausting and miserable. When we find joy in our work Today, it does not matter what comes of it. In this way, making goals can keep us motivated toward steady progression. We want to enjoy the race, not become so focused on the finish line that we despise every step. Today is the springboard for tomorrow. If we jump Today, we can fly tomorrow, but we have to jump first. Fixating on the desire to fly will not make it happen. The true happiness is Right Now.

Death

> You may delay, but time will not.
> – Benjamin Franklin: Inventor and Writer [6]

We all die. Our lives could end at any moment. We look to the future as the "brighter day" and convince ourselves that death is a long way off. We sacrifice the present moment for a future that may never come. We justify our lack of activity in the present moment by living in the future or past.

No matter how much we deceive ourselves, time ticks away. Ralph Waldo Emerson said, "A day is a miniature eternity." [7] We often waste eternities because we feel like we have plenty of time to accomplish our dreams. Laziness causes us to live day-to-day in a lackadaisical, lethargic state, waiting for life to happen the way we expect it to, while over-work causes us to live miserably, striving toward goals and ambitions that do not make us happy. Both of these states believe that Today is the least important day on the calendar. When we waste our lives waiting for another day, we spit on this great gift of life.

> An awareness of the high stakes of mortality can resensitize a jaded person's sense of taste and life becomes a delicious meal no matter how basic the recipe.
> – Martin Prechtel: Writer and Mystic [8]

Our culture fixates on youth and vitality. We fear growing old and fear death even more. When we allow ourselves to realize our fragile natures, rather than run away from them, we understand the true importance of the current moment. We run away from the idea of death because it gives us infinite amounts of time to waste. If we focus on death instead, it does the opposite.

> Death gives meaning to our lives. It gives importance and value to time. Time would become meaningless if there were too much of it.
> – Ray Kurzweil: Writer and Inventor [9]

If this moment is the only one we have, it becomes critical that we use it in productive ways. There is no time to waste. We know that *we are here Now*. Understanding that death is a step away brings more meaning; it makes each moment more important.

We do not want to fixate on or fear our deaths, but we want to be aware that every moment could be our last. Consciousness shifts our frame of reference to Right Now. We can constantly ask ourselves, "What am I doing Now, with my last moments on Earth, and why?" This new perspective puts us in a place of power to take action.

Right Now

> The miracle is not to walk on water. The miracle is to walk on the green Earth in the present moment, to appreciate the peace and beauty that are available now.
> – Thich Nhat Hanh: Buddhist Monk and Writer [10]

When we only have Today for comparison, we realize the True Beauty of this moment and we are free. If we make a habit of accepting and finding happiness in the present moment, we are in the habit of doing so, and therefore in the future we accept and find happiness as well. It is the acceptance of what is happening Right Now that brings happiness.

There is a great deal of joy in the Now. I mean Right Now. As you read this, as I write this, as we both *exist*, there is happiness. When we are mindful of the present moment, we understand that each of us is alive. It is easy to see how extraordinary life is when we look at Right Now and stop comparing this moment to others. "Comparison is the thief of joy." [11]

We are alive, and we have all that we need to be alive *here*. There is no fear, worry, or hate. There is simply this profound moment that surrounds us and it is beautiful. When we are not distracted, we can feel the True Beauty of this very second that we are sharing and co-creating.

Happiness is not a matter of having all that we want; it is a matter of being happy with all that we have. When we focus on the current moment, we realize all the great gifts we have and what brought us here safely. There is no need to do or have anything else because all that is required is already *here*. Each of us is a constantly flowing and changing river. We have a source and we have an end destination, but for now we are just babbling brooks at peace.

When we learn to accept what *is*, rather than expect it to be a different way, we can be conscious of all the voices that go on in our minds. Whenever we realize that we are somewhere else, we can choose to come back to the present and enjoy True Bliss.

Awakening into our True-Selves

> Your inner purpose is to awaken. It is as simple as that.
> – Eckhart Tolle: Spiritual Teacher and Writer [12]

Conscious living gives us the awareness to work with and find peace with our egos, rather than fight against them. One of the misguided ego's most powerful tactics is to distract us from Now. When we do not pay attention, the ego convinces us that it *is* us, and then we do not put up any arguments about its methods.

We want to be present at all times, rather than let our thoughts dictate when we will be thrown into a flashback or a flash-forward. As we learn to work with our egos, it becomes easier to enjoy the True Beauty of this Holy Moment.

We tend to focus on final results and forget about the path that leads there, but it is the quest that brings the most amount of fun! In *The Hobbit*, we read about Bilbo's *journey*. The book concludes when his journey ends. It is the quest that excites us. The final destination for life is death, and we seem to be in a great rush to get there, forgetting about our journey.

Consciousness guides us to act as our true-selves, because our true-selves are always conscious. Our true-selves are the unconditional acceptance that flows from moment to moment. The more aware we become, the more of our true-selves we experience.

As we become present, we live from our hearts and act in ways that bring happiness naturally. This means that our lives form into joy and excitement with ease as we simply live. We attain an effortless mastery over our lives.

In the quest to love and accept ourselves, our primary goal is to attain consciousness in each moment; this is what is meant by "awakening:" we are awake and present in each moment to make active and conscious decisions about it. Anything that distracts us from our true-selves, no matter how great it seems, leads to unhappiness. Consciousness keeps our egos in check so we can act in the interest of our true-selves.

Consciousness causes us to work toward our dreams, because our egos get out of our way. When we focus on our ascending awareness, we find our lives reshaping around us, as we simply enjoy them. Life becomes effortless and we create a series of moments that string together into a beautiful and wonderful life. A healthy relationship with the ego allows us to remain conscious, creating happiness for the entire world.

In order to remain present, remember the three A's: Awareness, Allowance, and Acceptance. Be *aware* of what happens, *allow* it to continue, and *accept* this moment. Applying these to ourselves and the world alleviates unnecessary suffering and empowers us to shape our lives and experience True Beauty.

Meditation to Mindfulness

> Be Here Now.
> – Ram Dass: Writer and Mystic [13]

Traditionally, the best way to attain consciousness is through dedicated meditation. Meditation helps us to stop the distractions of the mind and sit in this moment fully. It allows us to experience our true-essence as it *exists* and helps us to halt all of our external fixations.

We meditate to discover inner-silence and our inner-selves. Once we have found this, we can bring this consciousness to our daily lives. We can bring our meditation practice into every moment.

Conscious breathing, yoga, conscious living, walking meditation, and eating meditation are all methods that have been used to remain mindful of this moment. No matter which technique or methods are used, the purpose of all of these are to bring us back into our true-selves, and therefore back into that all-pervasive, all-accepting nature that we truly *are*.

> There are no ordinary moments.
> – Dan Millman: Writer and Public Speaker [14]

It does not help if we meditate for twenty minutes and then abandon what we have learned the moment we walk out the door.

We can apply the silence we find in meditation to Right Now and *live in consciousness*. This takes practice. Just keep breathing.

Practice!

1. Meditate. Every day. Stop making excuses. This one practice will change your life and make all other goals easier and more enjoyable.
2. This moment is perfect.
3. You might die tonight. Ponder this for a while. How does this thought affect your actions in the present?
4. Practice conscious living. Can you feel yourself breathe as you read this book? As you do the dishes? As you work? Feel your breath every time you think of it.
5. Find reminders for consciousness: "Driving reminds me to focus," "The wind reminds me to breathe," etc. Shift to mindfulness whenever you think of it.
6. **Questions:**
   Is there a difference between consciousness, mindfulness, awareness, sentience, and presence?
   Do we stop breathing when we are not aware of our breath?
   What is death and what does it mean?

10. BALANCE

> Happiness is not a matter of intensity but of balance
> and order and rhythm and harmony.
> – Thomas Merton: Writer and Mystic [1]

Life is overrun with work, sleep, play, relaxation, exercise, social activities, personal time, meals, errands, family, goals, and ambitions; finding balance seems impossible. We are either too busy-exhausted or we are too bored-restless. Attempting to make it all even-out is a battle that seems never-ending.

We have ample amounts of hours and days to do and be all that we want to, but the way we balance our lives leads to difficulty. We shift from one extreme to another and cannot find the easy path that leads to steady progression.

Living in balance can be viewed as a pendulum swinging back and forth. We find ourselves swinging between two extremes attempting to find harmony. Perhaps we feel lazy, so we push ourselves to do more, then we get exhausted and need a break again.

Or perhaps we eat too much, so we go on an extreme diet, only to "fail at it." When we live like this, we yo-yo between two polar opposites.

Extremes feed off of each other. Like the pendulum, the amount we swing forward is equal to the amount we swing backward. The more we try to force one pole, the more we create the need for the other pole. Sometimes we can push ourselves for an extended period of time, but we crash eventually. It is not possible to stay at one side for too long. If we stay up all night drinking, we have to spend the next day recuperating. If we devote a lot of energy to work, then we experience a time of exhaustion. Students study endless hours for finals week and then crash the moment the last test is over. When we create one extreme, the opposite also manifests. No matter what, life stays in balance.

The more extreme one pole is, the more extreme the opposite. These strong periods of growth and relax can lead to stress, anxiety, and depression, because we swing erratically from pole to pole. Some people may enjoy this type of balance, but most of us just find ourselves depleted.

Ego's Imaginary Poles

> When carried to extremes, opposites meet.
> – C.G. Jung: Founder of Analytical Psychology [2]

The extreme poles that we strive for are non-existent. When we balance in the middle, we see that there are no poles. There is no hot or cold when we look at a thermostat; it is all just temperature. Yet, if we label one side as hot, then we have to give a name to the other side. Once we invent one pole, it creates the other pole.

> In the sky, there is no distinction of east and west;
> people create distinctions out of their own minds
> and then believe them to be true.
> – Teaching of Buddhism [3]

There are no poles unless we create them there; these misperceptions create a lot of suffering. We see black and white, me and you, alive and dead, cold and hot, but these are created distinctions by the human mind.

All that we have discovered of existence is made up of energy. This means that everything we experience is the same; it is all vibrating energy. In communicating with one another, labeling opposites can be useful, if we know that in Reality they do not exist.

There is no separation other than what we create to be there. The first law of thermodynamics tells us that energy is neither created nor destroyed; it is only transferred. Even the difference between life and death is a mere energy transfer.

Infants do not see these distinctions. After a few years of rigorous training we learn to label things as separate from each other: square from circle, red from green, past from present, mine from yours. We find it useful to label objects in our relation to each other, but each time we create a distinction, the "opposite" is also created. "That is a chair," so everything else is "not a chair."

If we abandon our fixation on one extreme, the opposite blends into it and the line that divides them disappears. There is no east and west, there is only sky. There is no sky and earth; there is only energy. When we abandon our attachment to a particular idea, we stop forcing it into being.

We live Polar Lifestyles because the ego likes extremes. We are accustomed to the idea that some results are "better" than others. The ego fixates on an idea, and since it must always be The Best, it strives to achieve the most severe form of it. We see a skinny model and attach to that extreme, resulting in unhealthy dieting and starvation techniques. We see a body-builder and believe we are inadequate unless we also have a steroid-pumped, muscle-built body. Both of these ideas rely on extreme behavior that balances erratically.

We have trouble abandoning our labels because we fixate on imagined opposites. We label some results as "good," while the alternative is "bad;" when we create these poles, we attach to both. The more we try to force the one pole, the more the opposite is created and the harder we have to fight to escape it. We think that if we "try harder" that we will escape the "bad stuff." What we do not realize is that by forcing only the "good stuff" we create the need for the "bad stuff" to maintain balance.

The harder we fight against balance, the more it fights us. The more we resist, the more difficult life becomes. We struggle and strive for one extreme, but eventually we cave in and the pendulum swings backward. This causes us to be upset, because we attached to the other pole, so we attempt to force it into being again, resisting the nature flow of energy.

A misguided ego distracts us from what our true-selves want by convincing us to live its way: a Polarized Lifestyle. We dedicate tons of energy to the ego's ideals, which then exhaust us too much to find happiness in the current moment. Ego-desires manifest chaotic extremes, while heart-desires manifest acceptance and ease.

Duality and Oneness

> In love all contradictions of existence merge themselves and are lost. Only in love are unity and duality not at variance. Love must be one and two at the same time.
> – Rabindranath Tagore: Nobel Prize in Literature [4]

Science, religion, and philosophy have attempted to explain duality and oneness for ages, but for some reason we still struggle to understand them.

The yin-yang is a classic symbol for oneness, duality, and balance. It illustrates that though there appear to be opposites, they are both part of the same whole. Polar opposites may seem to be opposing each other, but they are actually connected and dependent. If there is a yin, then there has to be a yang.

The world is both dual and one, like the yin-yang. There are opposite poles, but they are part of the same whole. There is "east" and "west," but it is also just "sky." We can choose to view the world in a duality with opposing forces, or we can choose to view the world in oneness with one force (energy). Both are accurate.

It is sometimes difficult for us to comprehend that something can be two seeming-opposites at the same time, but life is full of paradoxes: wave-particle duality in quantum physics shows us that light moves as both a wave and a particle; Schrödinger's cat is both alive and dead; the body is trillions of life-forms and one life-form at the same time. Likewise, both duality and oneness are accurate.

We experience duality because of the ego. We want to view ourselves as separate from others and duality allows us to do so. If we shift and view all existence as energy, we can see that everything is the same. *Existence* is in balance with itself, ebbing and flowing. There is no separation between us. Most of our atoms are empty space, so even the difference between me and you is just a little empty space.

We struggle to understand what it means for us to all be one. We are used to the dual nature of the world—seeing objects as different from ourselves—but there is no difference between our internal world and our external world. It is all energy.

There are many different diagrams, moulds, and patterns we can use to explain oneness, but religion, spirituality, science, and philosophy have all tapped into it. In fact, oneness is an old idea that we have recently abandoned in favor of duality.

Almost every major religion has explained God to be all that *is*. Hinduism explains Brahman to be the eternal, unchanging, and infinite essence that makes up all matter, energy, time, space, being, and everything beyond in this Universe. [5] This same description is applied to God, Allah, and Yahweh.

> **Christianity:** Jesus said, "The kingdom of God does not come with your careful observation, nor will people say, 'Here it is,' or 'There it is,' because the kingdom of God is within you." [6] How can one place be within all of us unless we are somehow unified?

Hinduism: "The moon is one, but on agitated water it produces many reflections. Similarly, ultimate reality is one, yet it appears to be many in a mind agitated by thoughts." [7] There is one Reality, and it continually reflects itself.

The Higher Self (i.e., Higher Consciousness, God-Self, Buddha-Nature, Christ-Consciousness, or God-Consciousness) is a concept that has also been passed among many religious traditions. The Higher Self can be described as the God within each of us. Not to say that we are all gods, but more so that we are all part of that Highest Being. This concept of the Highest Self (God) encourages the idea that we are all facets of One Divine Being. Higher consciousness has been discussed in Buddhism, Jainism, Sufism, Hinduism and some Christian sects.

Recently, even science has gotten behind this idea of oneness. Quantum physics shows that when photons, electrons, or molecules are split apart, they are still connected (i.e., quantum entanglement). When one pair is altered, the other is affected, even when they are separated by hundreds of miles. [8] It is possible that this example is a microcosm for the Universe. When one person (energy) is affected, it affects people (energy) that are far away, just like the photons, electrons, and molecules. We are all part of the energy that exploded out of the Big Bang. It is not much of a stretch to realize that even though we are now "separate," we are still part of that original creation, just like quantum entanglement.

We can also see the concept of oneness illustrated in nature. The Great Barrier Reef is not a plant; it is the exoskeleton of billions of polyps. These creatures are known as the largest organism on Earth; they are one and dual. Each polyp has its individual experience, but the whole system functions as one. We also describe the hive mind of insects and fish to explain their seeming ability to function as one unit. In nature, complex systems like this are typical. It is not uncommon for the destruction of a single species to take down an entire ecosystem. Though we appear separate, we are much more interconnected than we like to admit.

Duality helps us ponder the nature of ourselves and what *exists* around us. We can use this view, as long as we understand that all of us are connected. When we ignore this fact, it is easy to destroy others in our ignorance of how it harms ourselves.

There is still much to learn and ponder about oneness, but we do know that the Universe always remains in balance, because there is not another option. Everything just *is*. It shifts, flows, and changes, but it always *is*; energy is neither created nor destroyed. When everything is One, the distinctions between poles disappear and we can flow in the natural harmony without fixating on one extreme.

Finding "The Middle Way"

> Life is like riding a bicycle. To keep your balance you must keep moving.
> – Albert Einstein: Nobel Prize in Physics [9]

It does not make any sense to attempt to achieve extremes. A polar opposite creates another polar opposite and this creates struggle and hardship. If we let life flow as it *is*, we are free to ride the waves wherever they take us; we accept whatever happens without attaching to one side.

There is a free flow and transfer of energy that occurs in the Universe: "For every action there is an equal and opposite reaction." [10] Everything ebbs and flows; everything changes. Knowledge of this concept makes life effortless and easy; we never have to fight or force our agenda. Force is met with an equal force. There is no point to pushing, because it will be met with an equal, opposing push.

We want to avoid force, but we can still work toward goals and ambitions. We can use balance to make steady growth while maintaining happiness in ease and flow. There are three concepts that can help us release ego extremes and come to rest in the middle:

Simplicity: Reduce unnecessary things, people, ideas, and situations. Cleaning up these distracting fragments gives us the time and energy to focus on what we want. Juggling is easier with three balls than with twenty. Fewer distractions help us narrow our minds to a single focus. Have the single-mindedness of a river that aims at the ocean.

Moderation: Take just enough: no more, no less. Eat just enough to feel satisfied; work just enough to fulfill needs; play just enough to feel happy: everything in moderation, including moderation itself. Allow your waters to flow freely down the mountain; no need to rush or overindulge.

Diligence: Steady effort and commitment can help us to accomplish our heart's desires. Do not mistake diligence with obsession, but work slow and steady toward a committed task. A river does not give up; it works a little every day until it accomplishes its goal.

Through simplicity, moderation, and diligence, the rain from the highest peak reaches the ocean. Have one goal, work steadily, and do not give up. It is a long journey, but the water remains at peace throughout.

Staying in balance in the middle of ease and flow is what Siddhartha Gautama taught as The Middle Way. This is the path between the extremes of sensual indulgence and self-mortification; he explained balance as the way to liberation and Nirvana. Rather than try to push intensities, we can rest in balance—not too much and not too little. Since one extreme causes the other, we can stop the drastic behavior by avoiding creation and participation in intense poles.

The fable of *The Tortoise and the Hare* illustrates the two different types of balance. The Hare sprints for most of the race, but then needs a break just before the finish line. The Tortoise walks steadily toward the end and wins the race. With slow, steady progression, we can reach many goals. When we attempt to sprint, we need a break. The Middle Way allows us to be happy while also accomplishing our heart's desires.

Peaceful Balance through Acceptance

> Whisper words of wisdom: Let it be.
> – The Beatles: Music Group [11]

As we learn to accept ourselves and the world as it *exists,* Right

Now, we release the need for pushing extremes. Life is effortless and easy, if we let it be. Acceptance and love bring happiness with the least amount of effort.

When we attach to external sources, we become painfully aware when there is a lack of them. For example, when we want to be with someone, we attach to the idea of being with them, and are more likely to notice when they are not there. If we do not attach to them, it does not make a difference whether they are or not, we just enjoy when they are there.

Healthy balance is easy; it is the natural state of life. It is when we resist that it gets difficult. When we learn to let go of our need to force situations a certain way, the world unfolds before us in the most balanced and beautiful way imaginable. When we accept our true-selves, the extremes fall away on their own.

There is no use making ourselves miserable over an extreme. All is well. All is perfect. "Follow your bliss." [12]

Practice!

1. Simplify all aspects of your life.
2. Practice moderation. Pick one or two areas at a time until you master them.
3. Learn to work diligently toward a single goal while maintaining easy balance in all aspects of your life.
4. Make a list of extremes that you fixate on, (e.g., I hate cold, I need money, I hate housework, I want a relationship, etc.). Notice how fixations create opposites in your life.

5. **Questions:**

    What is balance?

    How does your worldview (unity, duality, trinity, quaternity, etc.) influence your experience?

    What are opposites and why do they exist?

11. ALONENESS

> There are those among you who seek the talkative through
> fear of being alone. The silence of aloneness reveals to
> their eyes their naked selves and they would escape.
> – Kahlil Gibran: Poet and Writer [1]

Loneliness and aloneness are not the same. Loneliness is a depressive feeling of longing for company; it is based off of the desire for companionship. Conversely, aloneness has no emotion tied to it; it is the awareness of solitude. According to Osho, "Loneliness is always concerned with others; aloneness is concerned with oneself." [2] When we are alone, we either experience aloneness (accepting), or loneliness (rejecting).

Conscious aloneness is healthy; it helps us practice being our true-selves. The more aware of ourselves we are, the more we take an active role in our lives. On the other hand, if we ignore ourselves and seek to find other people to fill a void within us, we feel lonely, empty, and isolated.

We spend a lot of time alone, but very little time in aloneness. Technology allows us to spend time isolated, while also ignoring and losing ourselves. With the mind distracted in gadgets, we neither connect with others nor ourselves. We have discovered the new concept of being "alone together." We are able to be in a room with others, while being lost somewhere else. In this fashion, we forget ourselves as well as those around us.

The less we connect with ourselves, the more isolated within we feel. Then, we fear real human interactions, because we are afraid to share ourselves. For many, we join together to consume and experience, but we do not create bonds or share ourselves with each other.

Fear of Self

> Which is worth more, a crowd of thousands,
> or your own genuine solitude? Freedom, or
> power over an entire nation? A little while alone
> in your room will prove more valuable than
> anything else that could ever be given you.
> – Rumi: 13th Century Sufi Poet [3]

Loneliness is the fear of being alone with ourselves. Being alone is dangerous to an unhealthy ego's fragile state because there is nothing to distract from the rising subconscious thoughts. The ego invents the fear of being alone to prevent us from releasing our repression.

The misguided ego discourages meditation, silence, aloneness, and relaxation because we become aware of our true-selves in these moments. Even a solitary moment of peace reveals thoughts that the ego is holding back. If we catch on to even one of these thoughts, the ego's spell is broken.

The more corrupt the ego becomes, the more we fear being alone, silence, and stillness. The more lies we tell ourselves, the more fearful the ego gets that it will be discovered. Hiding our true-selves is one of the primary purposes of the misguided ego, and therefore, loneliness is one of our strongest fears. There are a few tactics the ego uses to avoid being alone:

> **External Distractions:** We avoid living within our bodies; we live on the outside, experiencing life through what we touch, smell, see, hear, and taste.
> **Endless Chatter:** If we constantly talk, there is no time to delve inside. We chatter externally to run away from any internal voices and sensations.
> **Boredom:** In boredom we perceive our minds, so we fill up our lives with stuff to avoid hearing the voices and feeling emptiness.

These ego games work to some extent, but when we continually run away, we lose ourselves. Our self-relationships grow weak when we never spend time alone strengthening them.

Loneliness is caused by an unhealthy relationship with ourselves. Many of us no longer take the time to get to know ourselves and feel lost because of it. When we disconnect from our inner-selves, we cannot answer basic questions like, "What do I like to do?" "What do

I want to do with my life?" or "What are my ambitions?" We spend so much time running away that we forget who we *are*.

We desire other people to spend time with us, but we do not want to spend time with ourselves. We crave love from other people, but we do not show ourselves the same courtesy. Rather than take the time to know ourselves, we fill up our emptiness with unnecessary timewasters. Many of us do not realize that our inner-selves are missing, because we are so distracted in our external world. However, we inevitably find ourselves alone at some point and then we feel the loneliness of our absent selves.

We crave our inner-selves and yet we are afraid to go find them, so we rely on outer stimuli to distract us from our inner-demons. This is true to the extent that when people are isolated from familiar surroundings, they can get neurotic because they no longer have an external source to blame for internal pain. [4] When we are alone for extended periods of time, we realize that our suffering is self-inflicted and we do not know how to cope.

We project our inner-demons upon other people, and when we face aloneness, we have no one to target but ourselves. Aloneness forces us to confront these inner-demons, because we are presented with the shadows that lie within us. We think the way to escape our inner-darkness is by running from it, but like all fears, we dissolve them by accepting and loving them.

We fear soul-searching because we imagine the inner-landscape as some sort of purgatory where there are vicious inner-demons and very few sparkling lights. At first glance, this is a terrifying scene and we would rather escape and listen to our egos than face it. We spend thousands of dollars in classes, workshops, and therapy to discover truths about ourselves, hoping to have someone else tell us the answers. Yet, it takes exponentially less time and energy to discover these answers by ourselves than to have someone else explain them to us.

It is scary to face the darkness inside of us. Yet, before we reach the quiet unification of our hearts and minds, there are damages, brokenness, and suffering to walk through. We are so afraid of this barrier that we spend great lengths to run away.

All of us can get to know ourselves, but many of us do not. We escape at any possible chance. We would rather "throw money at the problem" than spend the time alone to solve it. The remedy for loneliness is to spend more time alone. Simple.

Freedom is Within

> You can get help from teachers, but you are going to
> have to learn a lot by yourself, sitting alone in a room.
> – Dr. Seuss: Writer and Cartoonist [5]

Meditation and spending time alone help us find our true-selves. When we sit alone for extended periods of time, we have no other choice but to go within.

Every major religious leader spent time in solitude before they released their great works. Moses received the Ten Commandments while alone on the top of Mount Sinai for 40 days. [6] Siddhartha Gautama taught the Four Noble Truths after meditating under a fig tree for 49 days. [7] Jesus was in the wilderness for 40 days before he began to preach. [8] Mohammad received the Quran while meditating alone in a cave on Mount Hira. [9] These teachers brought back some of the most revolutionary thought that has ever existed after spending great amounts of time in solitude.

We can learn to bring our inner-selves out into the public view once we find them within. Group-think, social-patterns, and unconscious behavior make it difficult to be ourselves. When we consciously spend time alone, we tap into that essence within and then we can strive to be that person at all times. Once we have done this, all loneliness disappears, because we now have a friend that is with us in every moment.

When our inner-selves rise to the surface of our beings, we conquer the fear of boredom, loneliness, and emptiness, because these fears are perpetuated by a perceived lack of self. The more we love ourselves, the more we like being with ourselves, and the less lonely we are. When we lose ourselves, we search for someone else to be with us at all times and fulfill our needs. When we love ourselves, we can meet each other on an equal playing field as a mutual interaction of co-creation.

We latch on to things and people in the attempts to define ourselves, but it is the time that we spend alone that defines us. Integrity of character is formed by what we do when no one is watching. There is nothing external to ourselves that is a "part of us," or "who we are;" it all lies within.

> Although you make much out of 'my friends' and
> 'my relatives,' they cannot help you at birth or at death,
> you come here alone, and you have to leave alone.
> – Dalai Lama XIV: Spiritual Leader of Tibet [10]

The more people, things, and activities we crowd into our lives, the less free we are; we are slaves to stuff. Aloneness clears away all of these *things* and leaves room for our true-selves to come through; aloneness creates personal freedom that cannot be taken away, because it is a presence of self that lies within. Even if we are physically placed in chains, no one can rob us of the true-self within and True Freedom.

Peace, Patience, Contentment, and Serenity

> Within you there is a stillness, a haven to which you can
> withdraw at any time and be at home there.
> – Hermann Hesse: Nobel Prize in Literature [11]

Our true-selves are located in the quiet center of our beings; when we overcome our repressions, we find them there waiting patiently for us. It is this inner-silence that we have forgotten and crave in every moment. This inner quietude is the overwhelming and full state of being we seek.

The acceptance and understanding of our inner-selves is a calm humility and surrender that cannot be found in the external world. We find this stillness in ourselves when we move past the fear and delve in. Accepting our darkness, as well as our light, leads to a strong inner-self that is confident enough to reveal itself in our daily lives.

There is some degree of self that can only be found by spending time alone and meditating. When we sit in aloneness, without any external distractions, we learn to accept ourselves, regardless of what the ego chatters about.

Silence and patience develop when we experience personal stillness on a regular basis. As we learn to work with and understand ourselves, we drop the fear of self and loneliness.

Quiet solitude is extremely important for all beings. Mother Nature uses stillness everywhere. When we adopt the pace of nature, we learn patience, understanding, and acceptance. These are all qualities that help us love ourselves and others. Likewise, loving ourselves and others teaches us patience, understanding, and acceptance.

Our relationships with ourselves are like plants: when we water them they grow, if we ignore them, they die. We have to spend time with ourselves in order to grow as ourselves. For most of us, our current self-relationship is like a friend that we never see. Many of us have not seen ourselves since childhood. Children are content to play alone for hours *and* enjoy it. This is time they spend in aloneness, building relationships with themselves. Sometimes we forget how to do this as we get older and the plant of our self-relationship withers.

Our inner-selves are our best friends. They know all of our secrets, they cannot lie to us, and they will not leave us. If we become friends with this person, we cannot be lonely, because there is always someone with us. When we take time to develop this friendship, we form an unbreakable bond. If we instead run away and lose our inner-selves, it feels like something is missing, because it is.

We can study the profound teachings of gurus, but if we do not spend time alone, we cannot understand what they were trying to tell us. There is so much to learn from our inner-selves, but we cannot hear our inner-knowing when our egos scream at us. Aloneness brings consciousness within so we can experience the world as our true-selves, rather than as our ego-selves.

Aloneness is the feeling of silence and solitude *inside*. It can occur, regardless of where we are. Once we find ourselves and that inner-silence, the serenity of self is with us always. Searching for peace and happiness outside is pointless because we feel them within.

Peace and freedom are states of being that can be taken with us anywhere. If we can learn to hear the silence when we are in silence, we can then learn how to bring that silence into the chaos of daily life. Aloneness enables us to experience that state and master it.

Practice!

1. Do something for yourself every day. Enjoy a hobby, take a bath, meditate, cook a healthy meal, do yoga. Do anything that makes you feel like *you*.
2. Spend time alone. Television, games, radio, etc. do not count.
3. Run toward loneliness! When something makes you feel lonely, do it more. Do it until you conquer it.

4. Before you speak, THINK. Is what you are about to say:

    T – True

    H – Helpful

    I – Inspiring

    N – Necessary

    K – Kind

    If it is not, remain silent. The idea of awkward silence is an invention of the ego. Embrace the profound quiet nature of *existence*; it will lead you to profound inner-silence.

5. Find a few moments here and there for relaxation throughout the day. Relaxation reminds us to come back to ourselves.

6. **Questions:**

    Can we completely transcend loneliness?

    What is True Freedom?

    What is silence?

12. HONESTY

*To see the universal and all-pervading Spirit
of Truth face to face one must be able to
love the meanest of creation as oneself.
– Mahatma Gandhi: Activist* [1]

Honesty is one of the least rewarded virtues of our time. We hear "Honesty is the best policy," but what does that mean? We view honesty as, "telling the truth," and do not realize what is encompassed in honesty as a state of being.

According to Merriam-Webster, being honest means all of the following: "Free from fraud or deception: legitimate and truthful; genuine and real; humble and plain; reputable and respectable; good and worthy; creditable and praiseworthy; marked by integrity; marked by free, forthright, and sincere expression; innocent and simple." [2] Honesty is a much broader term than, "not telling lies."

Dishonesty includes: lying, fallacy (intentional and unintentional,) deception, misleading statements, white lies, flattery, slander, secrets, and exaggeration. Sometimes we let people assume something and do not correct them, while other times we purposefully say false statements to hide something; many are dishonest without even realizing it! All of these are dishonest, because we knowingly let a person misunderstand. When we do any of these actions, we do not seek Truth, because we allow ignorance and deception to persist. We perpetuate ignorance, which is non-acceptance, and non-love.

There are many excuses and ways to lie, but they all prevent us from being candid and real. Some reasons we lie are to:

Acquire: Dishonesty pays and we find ourselves lying in the attempts to acquire objects and people we desire. A traveling salesman might lie while looking us in the eyes, making up elaborate stories about children in Sudan. The salesman is rewarded when the lies work and has few repercussions when they do not.

Hurt: If the facts are not in place to slander someone, we can make up lies in order to discredit or hurt them. We may desire revenge or wish to smear an opponent, like in political campaigns. When we do this, we demean people and place ourselves "above" them.

Hide: The ego-self has facts that it wants to hide. It needs its false stories to maintain itself and we make up untrue statements to deceive people. If people ask us personal questions, it is easier to lie than to explain the truth. We "put on airs," act strong, hide our vulnerabilities, and fear others will exploit our flaws, so we lie. Secrets of any kind are not "genuine and real" or "humble and plain," they are an attempt to deceive.

Flatter: We tell white lies to avoid hurting someone. We perceive the truth as painful, so we say statements that are untrue in order to avoid it. Flattery and exaggeration are used to alter details. These are deceptions and lies, even if they are done from a place of kindness.

All of these "reasons" (i.e., excuses) for dishonesty come from a place of fear. There is no logical reason to tell a lie. If caught, we are discredited and it leads to anger and resentment.

We lie because we believe that the lie is a more favorable story than reality and the benefits outweigh the risk of getting caught. When we fear the repercussions of the truth, we are motivated to lie, because we want to escape. We fear what honesty brings, so instead of accepting it, we run away. Dishonesty is a way to escape what *is* and replace it with a fictitious world.

Lying is destructive, but we allow it for many reasons; advertising, business contracts, flattery, white lies, and exaggeration are all accepted forms of dishonesty. We want people to compliment us, we expect businesses to exaggerate claims, and we avoid the truth when it is "not nice." Honesty is no longer the best policy, especially if lying will achieve a desired result. The more we want, the more acceptable it is to lie to get it. The stronger our ego-selves are, the more they convince us to deceive to fulfill their desires.

World of Truth

> I believe that unarmed truth and unconditional love will have the final word in reality.
> – Martin Luther King, Jr.: Nobel Peace Prize [3]

Lies create a world where no one trusts each other. It seems normal that we deceive and we expect that other people deceive us in return. Yet, the more we lie, the more we live in constant fear that someone is "pulling the wool over our eyes," because our reality is a projection of ourselves onto others: as within, so without.

Dishonesty is so commonplace that we even distrust people who *are* honest; we think they have a hidden motive. We no longer take people at face value and we always look for what's going on below the surface.

A world of honesty sounds like a figment of imagination; it seems impossible. There are so many illusions and fallacies around us that we can barely imagine a world where everything is real and candid. Movies like *The Invention of Lying* (2009) make fun of a place where everyone is truthful. Hollywood, advertising, isolation of self, and many more aspects of our culture have shut down what a world of earnest truth looks like.

We believe that other people have to be honest first and then the world will be different. We justify lying to others because we "know" they lie to us. We believe that others are dishonest and then we are dishonest in response. We believe that Earth was a dishonest place before we were born, and there is no way to change it. Even more than that, we do not even want to change it, because we are very comfortable with our lies and do not wish to stop. We do not realize how much our lies impede and restrict us on a daily basis.

Lying is dishonest and it creates dishonest relationships. When we lie, we cannot relate to each other as human beings. We look at others as a "way to get something," and if there is not "something in it for us," we do not talk to each other. We do not look each other in the eyes and create true interactions. This overall fakeness contributes to the counterfeit-culture we now experience.

Honesty and trust start within each of us; they are lifestyle choices. We can either decide to be honest or not; there is no in-between phase. We cannot tell "mostly" truths and still be an honest person; the devil speaks in *mostly* truths.

The most effective lies start with a grain of truth. When we are honest *some* of the time, it is the same being honest *none* of the time. We think that as long as we are truthful most of the time, then that is enough. Yet, it is the times we are dishonest that we get an accurate picture of the devil that lies within us. Once we cross that barrier and allow ourselves to lie some of the time, there is no way to prevent ourselves from discerning when it is acceptable to be dishonest and when it is not. If we lie some of the time, we use truth to support our lies, quite a manipulative tactic.

We wait around for other people to be real with us and in the meantime we portray a fake-character on the outside, reflecting the same distrusting actions that we despise about others. The more we lie, the more habitual it becomes. As "compulsive liars" and "habitual liars," we find ourselves lying before we know the reason, or perhaps there is no reason. Regardless, the more we deceive, the more acceptable it becomes in our minds and the more we do it.

No matter how talented we are at deception, we give ourselves away. Body language has been attributed to as high as 93 percent of language. [4] This means that when someone is lying, we subconsciously know. Body signals like looking left, blinking fast, avoiding eye contact, shifting around, closed body frame, and fidgeting can all be examples of body language used when lying. Salesmen learn to keep strong eye contact, make firm handshakes, and avoid unnecessary movements, but no matter how much someone learns to counter-act the signs of lying, we subconsciously know.

When we shift to a life of honesty, we find our whole world shifts in response. People detect realness about us and respond with realness about them. Alternatively, when people detect our barriers, they put up their own. When we drop those walls, others follow suit.

The more honest we are, the more honest the world becomes, since it is a reflection of ourselves. Honesty gets us to stop fixating on our own lies and the lies of others.

Seekers of Truth

> The Truth is inseparable from who you are.
> Yes, you *are* the Truth. If you look for it
> elsewhere, you will be deceived every time.
> – Eckhart Tolle: Spiritual Teacher and Writer [5]

The great teachers of the world have preached Truth for as long as we have recorded them. Gandhi, born a Hindu, dedicated most of his life to the search for Truth, even subtitling his autobiography, "The Story of My Experiments with Truth." He explained Truth to be synonymous with God:

> I am being led to my religion through Truth and Non-violence (i.e., love in the broadest sense). I often describe my religion as religion of Truth. Of late, instead of saying God is Truth I have been saying Truth is God, in order more fully to define my religion. [6]

He also explained:

> An error does not become truth by reason of multiplied propagation, nor does truth become error because nobody sees it. Truth stands, even if there be no public support. It is self sustained. [7]

Truth is considered to be so important that Hinduism, Islam, and Christianity all made their Supreme Being equivalent to Absolute and Ultimate Truth.

> **Christianity:** The Bible has many quotes about seeking truth and living it. In Zechariah it says, "These are the things you are to do: Speak the truth to each other, and render true and sound judgment in your courts;" [8] Psalm says, "Send forth your light and your truth, let them guide me; let them bring me to your holy mountain, to the place where you dwell." [9] Jesus said, "The truth will set you free." [10]

Islam: The prophet Muhammad says, "Strive always to excel in virtue and truth," [11] and "Lying leads to vice, and vice leads to indecent acts, and if a person goes on lying, in the sight of Allah, he is named a liar." [12]

Buddhism: Siddhartha Gautama stated that "Three things cannot be long hidden: the sun, the moon, and the truth." [13]

"Truth" versus "truth"

> There may or may not be only one single absolute truth and only one single ultimate way of salvation. We do not know. But we do know that there are more approaches to truth than one, and more means of salvation than one.
> – Arnold Toynbee: Historian and Writer [14]

It is important to note the difference between Truth and truth. We each have our personal truths (lower case) that are real for each of us. Yet, there is an undeniable Truth (upper case) of what *is*, though it may be beyond the possibilities for our brains to comprehend. If we believe that our personal truths are the Truth, we fight and war with each other in the attempts to press our personal truths upon other people.

The Truth is what *is*, and therefore, everyone can agree with it—when we allow ourselves the freedom to discover it. If not everyone agrees, of their own accord and without force, then it is not Truth. This means that we have discovered very few Truths. We fixate on disagreeing with each other, rather than finding the commonalities between us and in this process, we drive ourselves further away from finding Truth.

We create models to explain Truth using our limited intelligence and concept of the world, and then expect it to be a perfect explanation for how life *is*. "If the human brain were so simple that we could understand it, we would be so simple that we couldn't." [15] Likewise, if *existence* were so simple that we could understand it, it would be so simple that we couldn't. It would serve the human race to move past our differences in personal truths and seek the Ultimate Truths together in solidarity.

There are many paths to get to the top of a mountain. Once at the top, they are all the same place, but we can climb it in many ways. The Bhagavad Gita says, "However men try to reach me [God], I return their love with my love; whatever path they may travel, it leads to me in the end." [16] Similarly the Rig Veda states, "Truth is one, but sages call it by different names." [17] The Sufi poet, Hakim Sanai, said, "The true core of truth goes beyond the terminology of 'How' and 'Why.'" [18] As soon as we allow ourselves the freedom to seek Truth, we are overwhelmed by the possibilities that there *are*.

Ignorance is a non-acceptance of what *is*, while honesty and truth are acceptance. Instead of spending our energies creating ideas that fall apart, we can spend our energy in our search for Truth. It requires all of us together to find the Answers. When we let go of our need to push our personal agendas, we can seek Truth together.

Honesty is Acceptance

> I prefer to be true to myself, even at the hazard of
> incurring the ridicule of others, rather than to be
> false, and incur my own abhorrence.
> – Frederick Douglass: Writer and Abolitionist [19]

When people lie to us and we lie to others, we fear showing our true-selves, because we distrust each others motives. The more we hide and lie from each other, the less we connect. This creates a sense of isolation, which makes it easy to continue to lie and manipulate to get what we want, since we believe that we do not care about anyone.

Lying hurts everyone involved. Rather than create acceptance and respect between each other, we create dishonesty and fear. Even if we "get something out of it," we lose the opportunity to connect with that person.

Dishonesty means that reality is not acceptable. We tell ourselves that the truth is "bad" and the lie is "good." For example: When we lie, exaggerate, or deceive in order to inflate ourselves, we are saying that our true-self is not as good as the false one.

We lie to repress the truth. In this way, dishonesty is a form of self-hate; it means we cannot accept the truth to the extent that we are willing to expend great efforts to hide it. We think it is easier to invent a new reality than it is to accept the current one.

When we lie, our egos must track it to prevent discovery, by others and ourselves. No matter how convincing and self-aware we think we are of our lies, the moment we say it, a part of us has to believe it, even if it is only for a moment. The longer we tell a lie, the more we believe it is true. Eventually, lying forces the truth into the subconscious in a form of self-repression. Carl Jung explains the side effects of lying:

> [A merely private secret] resembles a burden of guilt which cuts off the unfortunate possessor from communication with his fellow-beings. [20]

He further explains that lies branch off from the consciousness and create complexes in the unconscious. If we can keep our lies straight, some of this behavior can be avoided, but the more we tell a lie, the less aware we are of its untruth. [21]

The mind is unbiased; once we decide that lying is acceptable, it is acceptable in all situations. We think we can just lie to others, but honesty is a state of being. Dishonesty is an attempt to change the facts into ideas that serve us better. This non-acceptance of the world makes us dishonest, and our dishonesty with ourselves causes us to reject reality.

We are honest to the level that we practice honesty and acceptance of ourselves. The guilt and self-inflicted pain caused by lying is enough to torture a being. Acceptance is the key to loving ourselves, and we cannot do that when we are dishonest. When we practice dishonesty, we refuse to accept how life *is*, and therefore cannot *live in Love*.

We run away from honesty because the truth makes us uncomfortable. Revealing inner-truth to others means feeling vulnerable. Honesty sometimes means discussing sensitive and painful information and we believe it is easier to lie about it. We fear revealing the truth, especially about our vulnerabilities, because we think others will attack us for it. We are not comfortable enough with ourselves to admit the truth, so we lie to keep the truth covered up. We fear other people gaining the upper hand, so we keep all facts about our fragile human nature deep within us.

As we become comfortable with sharing the truth, becoming vulnerable, and sharing our secrets, we release the bonds that hold the self in the subconscious. The corrupt ego loves lies, because it can use them to fabricate false-facts about itself. When we stop doing this, the ego loses one of its most powerful weapons. *Without lies the ego has no power over us.*

We release guilt, self-hate, and non-acceptance when we stop lying and deceiving, because our true-selves are in a state of unconditional acceptance. We also free up our minds from the ego's clutches, because dishonesty takes up a lot of mental energy. There are a lot of ego voices that have to be put in place to maintain lies; when we stop lying, we silence all of them.

We cannot live as our true-selves if we are dishonest about who we are. This is part of why it is important to seek Truth. Through honesty we can seek to find the true state of Reality. Lies create a false-reality, and a false-self.

Vulnerability and honesty can be difficult, especially if we secretly believe people will take advantage of us. However, when we get in the habit of living our own truths, it is very difficult for someone to manipulate us. When we know our own truths, someone cannot convince us to go against them. The more honest and accepting we are with ourselves, the more real we are. We avoid the division of self that occurs when we hide part of ourselves and exaggerate other parts.

When we lose our true-selves to deceit and let people believe false aspects of ourselves, it is nearly impossible to accept our true-selves. We assume that no one will accept us, our methods, or our desires; because we already decided that we are not acceptable. Honesty is a form of accepting the truth and telling it, rather than not accepting and hiding it.

Imagination to Creation

> A man is but the product of his thoughts.
> What he thinks, he becomes.
> – Mahatma Gandhi: Activist [22]

Children use imagination as a form of play. We forget about this wonderful skill as we get older and become "realistic" about the world. We see "life" as it "really is" and stop creating and inventing in the current moment. While this "realistic" perspective may be a form of accepting the world, it also forms its own delusions. Our minds influence what we see and the "realistic" perspective is based on assumptions as much as any other worldview.

It is the power of imagination that gives us the capability to dream of new possibilities. After all, it was the imagination of Thomas Edison that dreamed up the light bulb. It was the imaginations of the Wright brothers that dreamed of human flight. It was the imagination of Gene Roddenberry (creator of Star Trek) that led to many of our current technological devices. All of these ideas were thought to be "unrealistic" at some point. If we believe in our imaginations, they color our world and literally change the place where we live.

In the quest for honesty, it is easy to get confused and shut down our imaginations, because they are not "real." We are taught to be "honest" about "what happened" and limit our imaginations. There could not have been a pirate attack at school, so we think our children are "lying to us."

There is a big difference between lying and imagination. Lying comes from a place of fear and deception. Imagination comes from a place of creation, inspiration, curiosity, and love. We could say that the Wright brothers were lying when they imagined flight, but we do not, because of the intention behind what they were doing. Imagining flight was the initial creation of an idea that was later brought about. When we use our imagination, we are in a state of creation and innovation.

> Imagination is the beginning of creation. You imagine what you desire, you will what you imagine, and at last you create what you will.
> – George Bernard Shaw: Nobel Prize in Literature [23]

Imagination is a form of idea generation and possibility creation. When we imagine an idea as feasible, it enters the realm of possibility in our minds and therefore becomes possible. Before we imagine an idea, our minds shut out the possibility for it to happen. Imagination creates a possibility so that we can make it happen. It is only when we first create an idea in our minds that it can ever enter into the physical world.

> I am enough of an artist to draw freely upon my imagination. Imagination is more important than knowledge. Knowledge is limited. Imagination encircles the world.
> – Albert Einstein: Nobel Prize in Physics [24]

Honesty and imagination go hand in hand. If we only speak in truths, and we speak of our imagination, then we can consciously create the physical world through speech. The more honest we are, the more power there is behind our words. This means that the power of our imagination becomes much stronger. Albert Einstein spoke of his imagined ideas, and he was taken quite seriously, because they were his truths even when they were imagined.

> Imagination will often carry us to worlds that never were. But without it we go nowhere.
> – Carl Sagan: Astronomer and Writer [25]

There is a balance between imagination and the physical world. Most of us forget our imaginations and fixate on our surroundings. Let yourself play and imagine great possibilities. If this is combined with a state of honesty and truth, you will create entire worlds. Imagination holds great power. Play with it and imagine a world worth living in.

Practice!

1. Stop lying. This includes white lies, deception, flattery, and exaggeration. All lies are lies. If this means you are in a situation where you cannot figure out what to say, remain silent. Silence is a powerful weapon and a shield.
2. If you catch yourself lying, admit it and correct it. Accept the repercussions for your lies. It will stop you from doing it in the future.
3. Deception is dishonest. If we know someone believes a fallacy and we do not correct them, it is the same as a lie, even if the misunderstanding was the other person's "fault." Fallacy perpetuates ignorance.
4. Be vulnerable. Find the lies you are most uncomfortable with and start telling people the truth about them. You will soon wonder why you cared so much.
5. Do not lie for other people, but avoid gossip as well. Encourage friends who lie to tell the truth.
6. Keep your promises. There is a lot of power in promises. If you never break your word, then making a promise is a guarantee that it will happen. Value your word.
7. Imagine something Today.
8. **Questions:**
   What is Truth?
   Does it benefit someone if we lie to prevent hurting them?
   What is the imagination?

13. PURPOSE

> Birdsong brings relief to my longing. I am just as ecstatic as they are, but with nothing to say. Please, universal soul, practice some song, or something, through me!
> – Rumi: 13th Century Sufi Poet [1]

Throughout our lives we are repeatedly asked the same question, "What do you want to be when you grow up?" When we grow up, we change our minds and the dreams of becoming an astronaut or a doctor fade away, replaced with more "practical" ideas of nine-to-five jobs, regular paychecks, and office work.

As adults, many of us dream of a steady job, steady income, starting a family, and owning our own homes. These are beautiful dreams, but we sometimes let our jobs and other people replace our reason for existence and we let our true-selves fade away.

Many of us cannot answer the question, "What is my purpose in life?" At some point, we either forget or cannot decide on an answer.

We then wander around without focus and tend to accomplish very little, while making ourselves very unhappy.

Finding a purpose can make life worthwhile. When we find, create, and give meaning to our existence, we feel fulfilled and stimulated. Yet, "Infinite Possibilities" is a scary concept and we resort to mimicking the actions of those around us, rather than taking time to discover our own paths. There are as many options for life as there are people on the planet, and that is scary!

Many of us have lost ourselves behind a false ego idea and defense mechanisms. If we can clear all the unnecessary stuff going on in our heads, we start to see what our hearts desire. When we love and accept ourselves, our true purpose in life reveals itself to us.

Philosophy has long discussed "The Meaning of Life," and we have yet to find the Truth of it. When taken beyond our personal truths, we cannot prove what the Answer *is*, but each of us can live in ways that are true for us.

The more we clear out our mental programming and patterns, the closer we get to our true-selves. We may not be able to answer The Meaning of Life, but we can create meaning within our own lives.

Personal growth is difficult, because it has to be done alone. This path is often rough and intense, but each day is more enjoyable than the last, even at its most challenging moments. This quest enables us to say, "Today is the best day of my life," each and every day. Finding our purpose is the whole reason for being here. When we clear away all of our troubles, ego, and mental blocks, we find ourselves, purpose, and meaning. This makes all of the trials worth it.

Primary, Secondary, and Tertiary Purpose

> You are here to enable the world to live more amply, with greater vision, and with a finer spirit of hope and achievement. You are here to enrich the world.
> – Woodrow Wilson: President of the USA [2]

Our **primary purpose** is consciousness and self-actualization. [3] We want to love and accept ourselves and learn to be aware of the voices in our heads. In the end, we only have ourselves. Nothing and no one else walks through the final doorway at death with us. No matter who we love in this life, we will face that final destination alone, just us and our conscience. Death, suffering, and fear become less scary when we find ourselves; we learn to stand strong and we gain a powerful ally.

Consciousness creates lives that perpetuate happiness and love, rather than lives that perpetuate our egos. As we learn to live in the moment as our true-selves, our other purposes fall into place. Connecting to the true-self allows us to hear our inner guidance and understand ourselves. From this space we can figure out what we want and why we are here.

Our primary purpose is the foundation of the pyramid. It holds up our secondary and tertiary purposes. The more attention and dedication we allow for this step, the stronger and more powerful our secondary and tertiary purposes become. It is a strong foundation of self that dictates our actions.

Once we have found ourselves, we can then work on our **secondary purpose:** heart-desires. These are wonderful because they give us a focus, enthusiasm, and joy for life. Our secondary purposes are what bring happiness and zest to our existence. They are the reason we wake up in the morning and the dreams that excite us.

Once we clear ourselves of blockages, our heart-desires light up brilliantly before us. Once we can feel our inner-self, our secondary purpose becomes extremely obvious. It is not even a challenge.

We have to know ourselves before we can know what makes us happy; likewise, we have to work with our primary purpose before we can discover our secondary purposes. When we find that place of love and acceptance within and know ourselves, we can discover inner-truth of what we want.

Without the ego blocking us, the secondary purposes for life come to the surface. These can be much simpler than the ideas we initially think of; some of them are: to exist, to learn, to love, to live, to be, to create, to nurture, to serve, to heal, etc. Most desires are a tactic to achieve one of these purposes. A doctor has a desire to heal; a scientist seeks to learn more about the world; a mother wants to nurture and spread love. When we clear away the ego, we can see our true heart's desires below and work toward them.

The **tertiary purpose** is how to apply our secondary purpose to serve the world. Once we figure out what makes us happy and drives us, we can then flip it and figure out how we can use it to bring happiness to others. If we desire to learn, how can we use our knowledge to benefit the planet? If we desire to love, how can we spread love in a way that benefits the growth and progression of all? When we discover ourselves (primary purpose) and our heart-desires (secondary purpose,) we find out how to serve our fellow beings (tertiary purpose).

By the time we reach this phase, we are ready to go out in the world and be active in it. We build a solid foundation in ourselves and our own lives, and we will not manipulate and push our agendas onto others. In this space, we can serve our fellow creations from a place of gratitude and respect. The service we can provide from this space manifests great results.

After spending so much time on the self and our own interests, there comes a time when our own personal gain is no longer a driving force. We no longer seek to be better than others or control them. Rather, we seek stimulation and co-creation from other intelligences to excite and progress our understanding of what *is*. At this point we can take the personal truths we have discovered and apply them to the growth of the world.

Many of us rush into this tertiary purpose because we want to distract ourselves from ourselves. We seek to heal others because we do not want to look at our own flaws. When we do this, we use and abuse others to serve our own interests. We run away from ourselves, and we build our foundations on uneven ground.

We want to hold off on our tertiary purpose until we solidify ourselves. This does not mean that we cannot help others, quite the contrary. Service to our fellow man encourages us to grow and can help with the primary and secondary purpose. Yet, if we use others as a reason to run away from ourselves, then we cannot help anyone. Even the help we think we provide is either in some sort of personal debt-system (e.g., I paid for dinner, so you owe me love), or an escape from ourselves (e.g., As long as you are happy, I am happy). Both of these systems do not help anyone and are not true service to our fellow man. This is why we cannot help anyone else until we first help ourselves. We cannot be sure of our motives and schemes until we understand our true-selves.

Once we have found ourselves, our driving force, and a way we can use it to help the world, we find True Bliss. This is the way we are intended to live: As a beautiful race of beings, striving and co-creating for the happiness of *all*. When we are of service to the world, as our true-selves, we are fulfilled. Living life selfishly and isolated is empty and boring. It is the freshness and innovativeness of others that challenges and rewards us.

It is important to focus on ourselves, but only in the broad scheme and understanding that it leads to the assistance of others. Otherwise, we are born, live, and die, and the world is the same. Through our continual evolution and progression we can make magic and create new worlds.

> To realize one's Personal Legend
> is a person's only real obligation.
> – Paulo Coelho: Poet and Writer [4]

In seeking a life purpose, we often complicate it up with detailed "plans" for how life will develop. We see ourselves in a very specific situation and decide that is the only possibility for our happiness. We then try to force this complicated plan into reality. What we do not realize with this is that the surreal ideas in the mind's eye do not make us happy. Even if we get what we asked for, verbatim, we are still unhappy. In fact, it can lead to increased unhappiness, because now we have nothing to hope for and to delude ourselves with.

Living our true purpose brings great joy. When we find our place and purpose, it is as if one more piece has been put into place in the world-puzzle. When we all align and find our places, the world functions as a healthy body, where we are each the cells, working in unison. When even one person is not free to function as they are intended, they block the natural flow of the world. One cancerous cell, dividing endlessly, can bring about the destruction of a multi-trillion celled creature. We each have a purpose, just like the cells of our bodies; the human race is the healthiest when we are all *free*.

Finding the Road to Freedom

> Just as the strong current of a waterfall cannot be reversed,
> so the movement of a human life is also irreversible.
> – Siddhartha Gautama: Founder of Buddhism [5]

Much of the journey on the road of life is finding the road. We second-guess ourselves and are afraid to "mess up." This causes us to live sheltered existences where we do not take risks and we do not achieve goals. We know that "Great gains require great risks," but we are so afraid of the journey that we forget to start. All it takes to accomplish your dreams is to begin somewhere. Pick a place and start, do not give up, before you know it you will be well established on your quest.

Do not be afraid to start small and work your way up. You would not eat an elephant in one bite, it takes many small ones. Work steadily toward your goals and one day you will find that all of your dreams have come true.

There is no way to "screw up" your life. There is no manual that gives the "correct" way to live. You may take unforeseen paths on the road, but it is the adventure that makes the journey worthwhile. The only way to screw up life is to never begin. You will have to work hard no matter what you do, but if you strive for your heart's desires, it will be worth the effort.

> The aim of life is self-development.
> – Oscar Wilde: Poet and Writer [6]

When we clear away all the dust gathering in our minds, we can see the true person that lies beneath. Once we each find ourselves, we find our secondary and tertiary purposes. The funny thing is: the minute we find ourselves, our secondary purpose comes screaming in from the subconscious, followed by the tertiary purpose. We know what to do and how to do it, because we have ourselves as a counselor. There is a purpose that we are each born to do, a job we are each perfect for, and if we can listen to ourselves, we hear the voice that tells us the answers. Emma Goldman said:

Only in freedom can man grow to his full stature. Only in freedom will he learn to think and move, and give the very best in him. Only in freedom will he realize the true force of the social bonds which knit men together, and which are the true foundation of a normal social life. [7]

When we live our lives in continual restriction, it is no wonder that we cannot discover our purpose in life. True Freedom is what lies within when we let our inner-selves free, and it cannot be taken away. As we free ourselves from our own mental, emotional, and physical chains, we start to see our real-selves emerge onto the great playing field of life. Once we become an active participant in the Game, we can learn how to play it well. It is in this space that we find our purpose.

> Emancipate yourselves from mental slavery;
> none but ourselves can free our minds.
> – Bob Marley: Songwriter and Activist [8]

We can change the world every day that we are alive. When we are complete in ourselves, we naturally make the small changes that shift existence. When we are happy and open to the world, we spread that joy a little bit at a time; each person that we come into contact with is affected slightly and they go on to affect someone else. *The world is only moments away from complete peace and happiness.* When we each decide that we are tired of suffering, we can leave it behind and join the multitude of others that already *live in Love*.

A new world starts with each one of us. When we live as

ourselves, (conscious, happy, and responsible,) we create a new world one day at a time. Step into life; it is full of beauty and creation. It is a lot of work, and we each have to address our inner demons and struggles alone, but once done the world transforms into a new place.

All of this is a promise. The world is different when you let it be. I am not making claims for a world without suffering or effort, and I am not claiming it will be easy. Yet, this world I explain already exists. Many live in it every day. When we learn to shift our vision to love and acceptance, the world shifts. Go find it. Find yourself. Find the world. Love yourself. Love the world. Your purpose awaits.

Practice!

1. Hold off on your secondary and tertiary purposes until you find yourself. It will come. Be patient.
2. When you have found yourself and discovered your secondary purpose, figure out how to express and create that purpose in the world. Your tertiary purpose will come once you have actualized your primary and secondary purposes.
3. **Questions:**
   Who decides your purpose?
   Are you happy?
   What activities make you lose track of time?
   If you were going to teach a class, what would it be on?

INCONCLUSIVE CONCLUSION…

Dear friends, let us love one another, for love comes from God. Everyone who loves has been born of God and knows God. Whoever does not love does not know God, because God is love. … No one has ever seen God; but if we love one another, God lives in us and his love is made complete in us.
– The Bible: 1 John 4:7–8, 12 [1]

Learning to love and accept ourselves can be difficult. We run away from ourselves for so long that we do not even know where to start. I hope this book helps you find a place to begin.

There are many ways and many answers in life and I do not pretend to know all of them; even my ideas are ever-changing. Self-love has made it easier to live as my true-self and help others to live as theirs. It is not the only path, and if it is not your path, I hope you find one that works for you. Yet, if your current way makes you suffer, perhaps try this way for awhile. If nothing else, maybe you will learn something that will help you find your own way.

> Believe nothing, no matter where you read it, or who said it, no matter if I have said it, unless it agrees with your own reason and your own common sense.
> – Siddhartha Gautama: Founder of Buddhism [2]

The answers lie somewhere within us. Be cautious of those that claim to have all the answers. Trust yourself and your inner knowing above all else.

When we attempt to bring Truth back from the Void, some of it gets lost in translation. We all understand the same truths, we just describe them differently. Rather than give you perfected answers, I want you to start asking questions within yourself. Through continual dialogue, acceptance, and discernment we can strive for Truth. Never stop asking questions. Find the child within that asks, "Why?" It is indeed the question that drives us.

> The ear tests words as the tongue tastes food.
> Let us discern for ourselves what is right;
> let us learn together what is good.
> – The Bible: Job 34:3–4 [3]

Through your quest, know that there is no end point where we become "enlightened." There is no point at which we stop all efforts to grow and progress. We are constantly in a state of arrival and departure, and it is in this place that we find The Answer. If you put enlightenment at the top of a mountain as a place you must travel toward, then you are putting a mountain between you and the answers. Quest forward and seek Truth, but know that you have already arrived and you are already *here*. The answers are within you.

The world is full of suffering and there are billions that legitimately need help. Unconditional acceptance gives us the desire to solve these issues and find answers to them. When we are stuck in the ego and its devices, we perpetuate the suffering of the world.

Self-love is a way to become part of the solution. When we are complete in ourselves, we stop contributing to suffering. The human race needs the healthy stability of all of its members in order to survive. It starts with each of us. We may never find a Utopia on Earth, yet it is certain that we will not if we do not have *you*. We do not have to do everything, but everyone can do something. Find what you are good at and commit to it.

Self-love does not end all the world's struggles automatically, but it is a viable answer, if we let it be. If an airplane is going down, it is wise to put on our own oxygen masks before we assist anyone else. If we do not help ourselves first, we cannot help others. Heal yourself, and then you will know how to heal other people.

I hope the spirit of love and acceptance encourages you to grow and become the best you can be in your true-self. I am excited to see who you truly *are* and what greatness you can accomplish. Realize that there are many people out there who are on a similar journey and that we are all just trying to find each other and connect.

There is a Love Movement going on across the whole world. Evidence can be found everywhere. You are not alone. Times change and the world changes. I hope you find your way to be part of that change and find your own path.

As I write these words, I feel each of you out there that read them through the time tunnel. I know that you can do it, and you will. You need only start. Love is a Force that can change this world. As Obi-Wan said, "Use the Force." [4]

Transform your world by transforming yourself. It starts with you. Suffering causes us to grow; do not run from it. Suffering is one of our greatest gifts.

> The flower that blooms in adversity is
> the most rare and beautiful of all.
> – Disney's Mulan [5]

Lastly, there are two questions that have been of great assistance to me on my quest of questions:

1. Does what I am doing make me happy, without hurting anyone else?
2. Is it helping me progress and learn?

If the answer to both is yes, keep it. If the answer to both is no, discard it. If it is split, then take no action. Between these two questions, we can assure that we are always happy and moving forward. From there, the rest is up to you.

Life is supposed to be fun. Do not get so wrapped up in self-actualization that you make yourself miserable. When times get hard, learn to laugh at yourself and the world. The Universe is a great Cosmic Giggle,[6] listen for it. Laughter is the best medicine and it can heal the world. Live. Laugh. Love. Find yourself and *be free*.

Journey on, traveler!

JOURNEY ON: INFLUENCES AND OTHER SOURCES

Isaac Newton said: "If I have seen further it is by standing on the shoulders of giants." [1] Find inspiration everywhere. These are some sources that were helpful to me. This list could literally go on forever…

Religious and Spiritual Texts

The Bible, The Quran, Bhagavad Gita, the many Buddhist texts, *Dhammapada, The Kybalion, The Vedas, The Upanishads, Tao Te Ching, I-Ching,* etc.

Books and Teachings by:

Thich Nhat Hanh, The Dalai Lama, Deepak Chopra, Mahatma Gandhi, Terence McKenna, Carl Jung… and many more.

Non-Fiction

Alex Grey – *The Mission of Art*

Benjamin Hoff - *The Tao of Pooh*

Dan Millman – *Way of the Peaceful Warrior*

Don Miguel Ruiz - *The Four Agreements*

Eckhart Tolle - *A New Earth* and *The Power of Now*

Louise L. Hayes - *You Can Heal Your Life*

Robert Anton Wilson - *Prometheus Rising*

Ram Dass - *Be Here Now*

Susan Gregg - *Dance of Power*

Novels

Hermann Hesse – *Siddhartha*

J.R.R. Tolkien – *The Lord of the Rings* and *The Hobbit*

Paulo Coelho - *The Alchemist* and *The Pilgrimage*

Robert Heinlein - *Stranger in a Strange Land*

Poetry

Hafiz – *The Subject Tonight Is Love*, translated by Daniel Ladinsky

Kahlil Gibran – *The Prophet*

Rumi – *The Essential Rumi*, translated by Coleman Barks

Documentaries

Ben Stewart – *Kymatica* (2009)

William Arntz - *What the Bleep Do We K(Now)?* (2004)

Don't Forget:

Yourself, Friends, Family, Nature, Science, Music, Art, Dance, Meditation, Community, Life, Love, Laughing, and the Universe.

REFERENCES

DEDICATION

1 Three Initiates, *The Kybalion*, (Yogi Publication Society, 1908), 2.

2 Hafiz, *The Subject Tonight is Love: 60 Wild and Sweet Poems* (Penguin Non-Classics, Jan. 2003), 47.

INTRODUCTION

1 Siddhartha Gautama, Quoted, Dalai Lama XIV, Author, *The Heart of Compassion: A Practical Approach to a Meaningful Life*, (Lotus Press, Oct. 2002), 47.

2 Paulo Coelho, *The Pilgrimage* (HarperOne, Sep. 2008), 163.

3 Andy Wachowski, Director, *The Matrix*, "Trinity," 1999.

4 Winston Churchill, *My Early Life: 1874-1904*, (Scribner, Jun. 1996), 60.

5 J.R.R. Tolkien, *The Fellowship of the Ring*, (The Random House Publishing Group, 1966), 278.

6 C.G. Jung, *Modern Man in Search of a Soul*, (Harcourt Harvest, Aug. 1955), 54.

7 Kahlil Gibran, *The Prophet*, (Alfred A. Knopf, Sep. 1973), 40.

8 C.G. Jung, Author, Gerhard Adler, Translator, R.F.C. Hall, Translator, *Psychology and Alchemy*, (Princeton University Press, 1970), CW 12, par. 126.

9 Lao Tzu, Author, Stephen Mitchell, Translator, "Sixty-Four," *Tao Te Ching: An Illustrated Journey*, (Frances Lincoln Limited Publishers, 2009).

10 Alex Grey, *Mission of Art*, (Shambhala, Mar. 2001), 26.

11 Jalal al-Din Rumi, Author, Coleman Barks, Translator, *The Essential Rumi, New Expanded Edition*, (HarperOne, May 2004), 246.

12 Hafiz (Hafez), Author, Robert Bly, Translator, *The Angels Knocking on the Tavern Door*, (HarperCollins, 2008), 33.

1. LOVE

1 Paulo Coelho, *The Witch of Portobello*, (Harper Perennial, Feb. 2008), 196.

2 Thomas Merton, *Disputed Questions*, (Houghton Mifflin Harcourt, Apr. 1985), 125.

3 Neale Donald Walsch, *Friendship with God,* (Berkley Trade, Oct. 2002), 315.

4 *The Living Insights Study Bible, New International Version,* (The Zondervan Corporation, 1996), 1 Corinthians 13:4-8.

5 C.G. Jung, *Modern Man in Search of a Soul,* (Harcourt Harvest, Aug. 1955), 18.

6 C.G. Jung, *Modern Man in Search of a Soul,* (Harcourt Harvest, Aug. 1955), 17.

7 C.G. Jung, *Psychology and Religion,* (Yale University Press, Oct. 1960), 93.

8 Robert B. Ewen, *An Introduction to Theories of Personality,* (Lawrence Erlbaum Associates, 2003), 22.

9 Alexander Pope, *An Essay on Criticism,* Lines 322-325.

10 Hafiz, *The Subject Tonight is Love: 60 Wild and Sweet Poems* (Penguin Non-Classics, Jan. 2003), 3.

11 Thich Nhat Hanh, *Teachings on Love: How Mindfulness Can Enhance Your Intimate Relationships,* (Sounds True, Incorporated; Nov. 2004), Track 1.

12 Mohandas Karamchand Gandhi, Quoted, Richard L. Deats, Author, *Mahatma Gandhi, nonviolent liberator: a biography,* (New City Press, Mar. 2005), 118.

13 Ben Stewart, Director, *Kymatica,* 2009.

14 Ben Stewart, Director, *Kymatica,* 2009.

15 Mohandas Karamchand Gandhi, *Gandhi An Autobiography: The Story of My Experiments With Truth,* (Beacon Press, Nov. 1993), 160.

16 Mohandas Karamchand Gandhi, Quoted by Arun Gandhi, Michel W. Potts, Author, *India – West* Vol. XXVII #13, (Feb. 2002): A34.

17 *The Living Insights Study Bible, New International Version,* (The Zondervan Corporation, 1996), Leviticus 19:18.

18 Original source unknown, attributed to both Katherine Mansfield and Dalai Lama XIV.

19 Siddhartha Gautama, Quoted, Thanissaro Bhikkhu, Translator, "Raja Sutta: The King" (Ud 5.1), *Udana of the Pali Canon,* www.accesstoinsight.org/tipitaka/kn/ud/ud.5.01.than.html (Access to Insight, Jul. 2010).

2. EGO

1 Martin Luther King, Jr., *Strength to Love*, (Fortress Press, 1977), 51.

2 Merriam-Webster, Definition of ego, www.merriam-webster.com/medical/ego (Merriam-Webster, Retrieved Oct. 2012).

3 Red Pine, *The Heart Sutra*, (Counterpoint, Aug. 2005), 48-70.

4 Eknath Easwaren, Translator, *The Bhagavad Gita*, (The Blue Mountain Center of Meditation, 2007), 39, 223.

5 Eckhart Tolle, *A New Earth: Awakening to Your Life's Purpose*, (Penguin Group, Sep. 2006), 59-61.

6 Sathya Sai Baba, "Quotes: God," www.saibaba.ws/quotes/god.htm (Sai Baba, Retrieved Oct. 2012).

7 Ben Stewart, Director, *Kymatica*, 2009.

8 Sun Tzu, Author, Thomas Cleary, Translator, *The Art of War*, (Shambhala Publications, Inc., 2000), 85.

9 Louise L. Hay, *The Power Is Within You*, (Hay House, Inc., Dec. 1991), Chapter 11.

10 *Guru Granth Sahib*, (Forgotten Books, 2008), Volume 1, 247.

11 C.G. Jung, Quoted, Edward Hoffman, Author, *The Wisdom of Carl Jung*, (Citadel Press, Feb. 2003), 147.

12 Eckhart Tolle, *A New Earth: Awakening to Your Life's Purpose*, (Penguin Group, Sep. 2006), 129-130.

3. FEAR

1 Franklin D. Roosevelt, "Only Thing We Have to Fear Is Fear Itself: FDR's First Inaugural Address," www.historymatters.gmu.edu/d/5057 (History Matters, Retrieved Oct. 2012).

2 Elizabeth Scott, M.S., "The Definition of Epinephrine," stress.about.com/od/stressmanagementglossary/g/Epinephrine.htm (About.com, Dec. 2007).

3 Oprah Winfrey, Quoted, Tuchy Palmieri, Author, *Oprah, in Her Words*, (Carl Tuchy Palmieri, Nov. 2008), 71.

4 Bruce Lipton, Ph.D., Ben Stewart, Director, *Kymatica*, 2009.

5 *The Living Insights Study Bible, New International Version*, (The Zondervan Corporation, 1996), 1 John 4:16, 18.

6 Hayim Halevy Donin, *To Be A Jew*, (Basic Books, Sep. 2001), 143.

7 Abdullah Yusuf Ali, Translator, *The Qur'an Translation*, (Tahrike Tarsile Qur'an, Inc., 2010), 2.112.

8 Stephen Mitchell, Translator, *Bhagavad Gita: A New Translation*, (Three Rivers Press, Aug. 2002), 4:10.

9 Siddhartha Gautama, Author, Thomas Byrom, Translator, *Dhammapada*, (Shambhala, Nov. 1993), 55.

10 Marie Curie, Quoted, Melvin A Benarde, Author, *Our Precarious Habitat*, (W. W. Norton & Company, 1973), v.

11 Carnegie Mellon University (October 10, 2007), "Stress Contributes To Range Of Chronic Diseases, Review Shows." www.sciencedaily.com/releases/2007/10/071009164122.htm (ScienceDaily, Retrieved Oct. 2012).

12 Siddhartha Gautama, Quoted, Dalai Lama XIV, Author, *Mind of Clear Light: Advice on Living Well and Dying Consciously*, (Atria Books, Sep. 2004), 99.

13 Robert Anton Wilson, *Prometheus Rising*, (New Falcon Publications, 2009), 48-51.

4. SUFFERING

1 Kahlil Gibran, *The Prophet*, (Alfred A. Knopf, Sep. 1973), 52.

2 Abraham Lincoln, Quoted, Orison Marden, Author, *How to Get What You Want*, (Thomas Y. Crowell Company, 1917), 74.

3 Jeremy E. Kaslow, M.D., F.A.C.P., F.A.C.A.A.I., *Neurotransmitter Repletion*, www.drkaslow.com/html/neurotransmitter_repletion.html (Jeremy E. Kaslow, Retrieved Oct. 2012).

4 Jennifer Bixler, CNN Medical Executive Producer, *More than 1 in 10 in U.S. take antidepressants*, thechart.blogs.cnn.com/2011/10/19/more-than-1-in-10-in-u-s-take-antidepressants (CNN Health: The Chart, Oct. 2011).

5 Deborah Kotz, Senior writer, *Do You Really Need That Antidepressant?* health.usnews.com/health-news/blogs/on-women/2010/01/06/do-you-really-need-that-antidepressant (U.S. News: Health, Jan. 2010).

6 Jeffrey Brodd, *World Religions: A Voyage of Discovery*, (St. Mary's Press, 2003), 13.

7 Bukkyo Dendo Kyokai, *The Teaching of Buddha*, (Bukkyo Dendo Kyokai, 1966), 38.

8 Jeffrey Brodd, *World Religions: A Voyage of Discovery*, (St. Mary's Press, 2003), 247-252.

9 Susan Gregg, *Dance of Power*, (IM Publishing, Sep. 2005), 142.

10 Oscar Wilde, *The Picture of Dorian Gray*, (Plain Label Books, Sep. 2007), 228.

11 Leonard H. Kapelovitz, *To Love and To Work/A Demonstration and Discussion of Psychotherapy*, (Jason Aronson, Inc., Jul. 1977), 66.

12 Vincent van Gogh, "Letter to Theo," (July 6, 1889).

13 J. Krishnamurti, *Total Freedom*, (Krishnamurti Foundation of America, 1996), 321.

14 Deepak Chopra, M.D., Quoted, www.eftuniverse.com (EFT Universe, Retrieved Oct. 2012).

5. DESIRE

1 Hafiz, *The Gift*, (Penguin Compass, Aug. 1999), 41.

2 Centers for Disease Control and Prevention, "Leading Causes of Death," www.cdc.gov/nchs/fastats/lcod.htm (CDC: FastStats, 2009).

3 Mark P. Mattson, Ph.D., "Neuroprotective signaling and the aging brain," www.ncbi.nlm.nih.gov/pubmed/11119686 (National Center for Biotechnology Information, Dec. 2000).

4 Kahlil Gibran, *The Prophet*, (Alfred A. Knopf, Sep. 1973, 72.

5 Deepak Chopra, M.D., Quoted, Mariana Bozesan, Ph.D., M.S., Author, *Diet for a New Life: 8 Steps to Weight Loss and Well Being*, (Sageera Institute LLC, Apr. 2007), 188.

6 Jalal al-Din Rumi, Author, Coleman Barks, Translator, *The Essential Rumi, New Expanded Edition*, (HarperOne, May 2004), 54.

7 Mohandas Karamchand Gandhi, *Gandhi An Autobiography: The Story of My Experiments with Truth*, (Beacon Press, Nov. 1993), 153.

8 Benjamin Franklin, *The Way to Wealth and Poor Richard's Almanac*, (Nayika Publishing, 2008), 24.

9 Abdullah Yusuf Ali, Translator, *The Qur'an Translation,* (Tahrike Tarsile Qur'an, Inc., 2010), 45.23.

10 Stephen Mitchell, Translator, *Bhagavad Gita: A New Translation,* (Three Rivers Press, Aug. 2002), 16.21.

11 *The Living Insights Study Bible, New International Version,* (The Zondervan Corporation, 1996), James 4:2-3.

12 Abdullah Yusuf Ali, Translator, *The Qur'an Translation,* (Tahrike Tarsile Qur'an, Inc., 2010), 29.62.

13 *The Living Insights Study Bible, New International Version,* (The Zondervan Corporation, 1996), Matthew 7:7.

14 Jeffrey Brodd, *World Religions: A Voyage of Discovery,* (St. Mary's Press, 2003), 52.

15 Dalai Lama XIV, *Advice on Dying and Living a Better Life,* (Atria Books, Nov. 2002), 87.

16 Osho, *The Art of Dying,* www.osho.com/online-library-allow-silences-joke-5f0b06d0-61e.aspx (Osho.com, Retrieved Oct. 2012), Chapter 6, 14.

6. IGNORNACE

1 John Milton, *Paradise Lost,* (Macmillan and Company, Limited, 1904), 91.

2 Jalal al-Din Rumi, Author, Coleman Barks, Translator, *The Essential Rumi, New Expanded Edition,* (HarperOne, May 2004), 252.

3 Richard Buckminster Fuller, R. *Buckminster Fuller on Education,* (University of Massachusetts Press, 1979), 130.

4 The Beatles, "Strawberry Fields Forever," *Magical Mystery Tour,* 1967.

5 Donald D. Hoffman, *Visual Intelligence: How We Create What We See,* (W. W. Norton & Company, 2000), 5-10, 23.

6 Robert Anton Wilson, *Prometheus Rising,* (New Falcon Publications, 2009), 28.

7 Robert Anton Wilson, *Prometheus Rising,* (New Falcon Publications, 2009), 33-43.

8 J.R.R. Tolkien, *The Hobbit,* (Random House Digital, Inc., 1982), 217.

9 Oscar Wilde, *Collected Works of Oscar Wilde: The Plays, The Poems, The Stories, and The Essays,* (Wordsworth Editions, Feb. 1997), 519.

10 Muhammad, Quoted, Abdullah Al-Mamun Al-Suhrawardy, Editor, *The Sayings of Muhammad,* (Kessinger Publishing, 2004), 90.

11 Hermann Hesse, *Siddhartha,* (Simon & Brown, Dec. 2011), 46.

12 Henry Major Tomlinson, *Out of Soundings,* (Ayer Publishing, 1931), 149.

13 Alex Grey, *Mission of Art,* (Shambhala, Mar. 2001), 10.

7. COMPASSION

1 Dalai Lama XIV, *Advice on Dying and Living a Better Life,* (Atria Books, Nov. 2002), 55.

2 Daniel Pinchbeck, *2012: The Return of Quetzalcoatl,* (Penguin, Sep. 2007), 330-331.

3 Hammurabi, Author, L.W. King, Translator, *The Code of Hammurabi,* (BiblioBazaar, Nov. 2007), 33.

4 Asghar Ali Engineer, *Compassion in Islam – Theology and History,* www.peaceforlife.org/resources/faithresist/2009/09-0100-compassionislam.html (Peace for Life, Jan. 2009).

5 *The Living Insights Study Bible, New International Version,* (The Zondervan Corporation, 1996), Matthew 5:7.

6 *The Living Insights Study Bible, New International Version,* (The Zondervan Corporation, 1996), Matthew 5:39-42.

7 Saint Mary's Press, *Understanding the Bible: A Guide to Reading the Scriptures,* (Saint Mary's Press, Jul. 2008), 65.

8 Rabbi Marc Gellman, Monsignor Thomas Hartman, "Exploring Religious Ethics in Daily Life," www.dummies.com/how-to/content/exploring-religious-ethics-in-daily-life.html (Dummies.com, Retrieved Oct. 2012).

9 Dalai Lama XIV, *The Art of Happiness: A Handbook for Living,* (Riverhead Hardcover, Oct. 2009), x.

10 Mother Teresa, "Mother Teresa Reflects on Working Toward Peace," www.scu.edu/ethics/architects-of-peace/Teresa/essay.html (Santa Clara University, Retrieved Oct. 2012).

11 Helen Keller, *Light in my Darkness,* (Chrysalis Books, Mar. 2000), 79.

12 Albert Einstein, "Letter of 1950," (New York Times, March 29, 1972).

13 David M. Rosen, *Armies of the Young: Child Soldiers in War and Terrorism*, (Rutgers University Press, January 2005), 57-64.

14 The United States Declaration of Independence, Paragraph 2, (1776).

15 Mohandas Karamchand Gandhi, *Gandhi An Autobiography: The Story of My Experiments With Truth*, (Beacon Press, Nov. 1993), 175.

16 Dalai Lama XIV, *Advice on Dying and Living a Better Life*, (Atria Books, Nov. 2002), 53.

17 Alexandre Dumas, *The Three Musketeers*, (Little Brown, 1893), Volume 1, 127.

18 John Donne, "No Man is an Island," *John Donne - The Major Works: including Songs and Sonnets and sermons*, (Oxford University Press, Jan. 2009), 344.

8. ANGER

1 George Lucas, Director, *Star Wars: Episode I – The Phantom Menace*, "Yoda," 1999.

2 Glenn R. Schiraldi, Ph.D., Melissa Hallmark Kerr, Ph.D., *The Anger Management Sourcebook*, (McGraw-Hill, Jun. 2002), 4-12, 39.

3 George Santayana, *The Life of Reason*, (Echo Library, Jul. 2006), 200.

4 Robert John McCrary, Ph.D., Psychologist, "Anger Management: A 'How-To' Guide," www.state.sc.us/dmh/bryan/webanger.htm (G. Werber Bryan Psychiatric Hospital, Columbia, South Carolina, 1998).

5 Mohandas Karamchand Gandhi, *Gandhi An Autobiography: The Story of My Experiments With Truth*, (Beacon Press, Nov. 1993), 74, 383-85, 388, 402.

6 Muhammad, Quoted, Abdullah Al-Mamun Al-Suhrawardy, Editor, *The Sayings of Muhammad*, (Kessinger Publishing, 2004), 87.

7 Rage Against the Machine, "Freedom," *Rage Against the Machine*, 1994.

8 Dalai Lama XIV, *Healing Anger: The Power of Patience from a Buddhist Perspective*, (Snow Lion Publications, 1997), 7.

9 Joan Borysenko, *Minding the Body, Mending the Mind*, (Da Capo Press, Nov. 2007), 189.

10 *The Living Insights Study Bible, New International Version*, (The Zondervan Corporation, 1996), Colossians 3:8, 12-13.

11 Aristotle, *Nicomachean Ethics*, II.1109a27.

12 Thich Nhat Hanh, "Thich Nhat Hanh on Loosening the Knots of Anger," www.shambhalasun.com/index.php?option=content&task=view&id=1756 (Shambhala Sun, Retrieved Oct. 2012).

9. CONSCIOUSNESS

1 Paul Coelho, *The Alchemist*, (HarperCollins, Apr. 2006), 29.

2 Deepak Chopra, M.D., *The Book of Secrets: Unlocking the Hidden Dimensions of Your Life*, (Three Rivers Press, Sep. 2005), 34.

3 Jane Austen, *Pride and Prejudice*, (RD Bentley, 1853), 323.

4 Original source unknown, Attributed to Winston Churchill.

5 Albert Einstein, "Interview on the Belgenland," (New York, Dec. 1930).

6 Benjamin Franklin, *Poor Richard's Almanac*, (CreateSpace, Apr. 2010), 60.

7 Ralph Waldo Emerson, *Journals and Miscellaneous Notebooks of Ralph Waldo Emerson, Volume 5*, (Harvard University Press, Jan. 1965), 142.

8 Martin Prechtel, *Secrets of the Talking Jaguar*, (Jeremy P. Tarcher, Aug. 1999), 31.

9 Ray Kurzweil, *The Age of Spiritual Machines: When Computers Exceed Human Intelligence*, (Penguin Non-Classics, Jan. 2000), 2.

10 Thich Nhat Hanh, *Touching Peace: Practicing the Art of Mindful Living*, (Parallax Press, Nov. 2009), 1.

11 Original source unknown, Attributed to Theodore Roosevelt, Dwight Edwards, and C.S. Lewis.

12 Eckhart Tolle, *A New Earth: Awakening to Your Life's Purpose*, (Penguin, Jan. 2008), 258.

13 Ram Dass, *Remember, Be Here Now*, (Hanuman Foundation, Oct. 1971), Introduction.

14 Dan Millman, *Way of the Peaceful Warrior*, (New World Library, 2000), 138.

10. BALANCE

1 Thomas Merton, *No Man is an Island*, (Shambhala Publications, Jun. 2005) 134.

2 C.G. Jung, *Modern Man in Search of a Soul*, (Harcourt Harvest, Aug. 1955), 41.

3 Bukkyo Dendo Kyokai, *The Teaching of Buddha*, (Bukkyo Dendo Kyokai, 1966), 52.

4 Rabindranath Tagore, *Sadhana: The Realization of Life*, (Macmillan, 1914), 114.

5 Jeffrey Brodd, *World Religions: A Voyage of Discovery*, (St. Mary's Press, 2003), 41-67.

6 *The Living Insights Study Bible, New International Version*, (The Zondervan Corporation, 1996), Luke 17:20-21.

7 *Maharamayana*, Quoted, Mike George, Author, *1,001 Meditations*, (Chronicle Books, Oct. 2004), 118.

8 Alexandra Witze, "75 Years of Entanglement," (ScienceNews, Nov. 2010), Vol. 178 #11, 25.

9 Albert Einstein, Quoted, Walter Isaacson, Author, "Letter to his son Eduard," (5 February 1930), *Einstein: His Life and Universe,* (Simon and Schuster, Apr. 2007), 367.

10 Sir Isaac Newton, "Third Law of Motion," www.thefreedictionary.com/Newton's+laws+of+motion (The Free Dictionary, Retrieved Oct. 2012).

11 The Beatles, "Let It Be," *Let It Be*, 1970.

12 Joseph Campbell, *Pathways to Bliss: Mythology and Personal Transformation*, (New World Library, Oct. 2004), xxiv.

11. ALONENESS

1 Kahlil Gibran, *The Prophet*, (Alfred A. Knopf, Sep. 1973), 60.

2 Osho, *The Psychology of the Esoteric*, www.osho.com/library/online-library-annihilated-positive-dream-72631feb-0da.aspx (Osho.com, Retrieved Oct. 2012).

3 Jalal al-Din Rumi, Author, Coleman Barks, Translator, *The Essential Rumi, New Expanded Edition,* (HarperOne, May 2004), 260.

4 Lilli 1956; Grunebaum 1960; Heron 1953, Quoted, Ben Stewart, Director, *Kymatica*, 2009.

5 Dr. Seuss, "On Becoming A Writer," (New York Times, May 21, 1986).

6 *The Living Insights Study Bible, New International Version,* (The Zondervan Corporation, 1996), Exodus 24:18.

7 Geshe Kelsang Gyatso, *Introduction to Buddhism An Explanation of the Buddhist Way of Life,* (Tharpa Publications, Jan. 2008), 8–10.

8 *The Living Insights Study Bible, New International Version,* (The Zondervan Corporation, 1996), Matthew 4:1-2.

9 Karen Armstrong, *Muhammad: A Biography of the Prophet,* (HarperCollins, Sep. 1993), 88.

10 Dalai Lama XIV, *Advice on Dying and Living a Better Life,* (Atria Books, Nov. 2002), 50.

11 Hermann Hesse, *Siddhartha,* (Simon & Brown, Dec. 2011), 71.

12. HONESTY

1 Mohandas Karamchand Gandhi, *Gandhi An Autobiography: The Story of My Experiments With Truth*, (Beacon Press, Nov. 1993), 504.

2 Merriam-Webster, "Definition of Honest," www.merriam-webster.com/dictionary/honest (Merriam-Webster, Retrieved Oct. 2012).

3 Martin Luther King, Jr., "Nobel Prize acceptance speech," (1964).

4 James Borg, *Body Language: 7 Easy Lessons to Master the Silent Language,* (FT Press, Sep. 2009), 18.

5 Eckhart Tolle, *A New Earth: Awakening to Your Life's Purpose,* (Penguin Group, Sep. 2006), 71.

6 Mohandas Karamchand Gandhi, *The Essential Writings,* (Oxford University Press, May 2008), 64.

7 Mohandas Karamchand Gandhi, *Young India 1924-1926,* (1927), 1285.

8 *The Living Insights Study Bible, New International Version,* (The Zondervan Corporation, 1996), Zechariah 8:16.

9 *The Living Insights Study Bible, New International Version,* (The Zondervan Corporation, 1996), Psalm 43:3.

10 *The Living Insights Study Bible, New International Version,* (The Zondervan Corporation, 1996), John 8:32.

11 Muhammad, Quoted, Philosophical Library, Author, *The Wisdom of Muhammad,* (Open Road Media, Nov. 2010), 402.

12 Muhammad, Quoted, Hazrat Abdullah bin Masud, Author, *Bukhari and Muslim*, www.iqra.net/Hadith/amal.php (Iqra Islamic Publications, Retrieved Oct. 2012).

13 Siddhartha Gautama, Quoted Anna Voigt, Author, Nevill Drury, Author, *A Way Forward: Spiritual Guidance for Our Troubled Times*, (Red Wheel Weiser, Jul. 2003), 110.

14 Arnold Toynbee, Quoted, *Britannica perspectives, Volume 3*, (Encyclopedia Britannica, 1968), 456.

15 Emerson M. Pugh, Harriet Griffey, *The Art of Concentration*, (Pan Macmillan, Feb. 2011), 12.

16 Stephen Mitchell, Translator, *Bhagavad Gita: A New Translation*, (Three Rivers Press, Aug. 2002), 4.11.

17 Rig Veda, Quoted, Shivesh Chandra Thakur, Author, *Religion and Rational Choice*, (Barnes & Noble, Jun. 1981), 114.

18 Hakim Sanai, "The Sufi," www.thesufi.com/sanai.htm (thesufi.com, Retrieved Oct. 2012).

19 Frederick Douglass, *Narrative of the Life of Frederick Douglass, An American Slave*, (Dover Publications, Apr. 1995), 19.

20 C.G. Jung, *Modern Man in Search of a Soul*, (Harcourt Harvest, Aug. 1955), 31-32.

21 C.G. Jung, *Modern Man in Search of a Soul*, (Harcourt Harvest, Aug. 1955), 31-32.

22 Mohandas Karamchand Gandhi, *Ethical Religion*, (Madras: S. Ganesan, 1922), Chapter 6, 61.

23 George Bernard Shaw, "The Serpent," *Back to Methuselah*, (General Books LLC, Mar. 2010), 89.

24 Albert Einstein, "What Life Means to Einstein: An Interview by George Sylvester Viereck," (The Saturday Evening Post, Oct. 26, 1929), 117.

25 Carl Sagan, *Cosmos*, (Random House, 1980), 4.

13. PURPOSE

1 Jalal al-Din Rumi, Author, Coleman Barks, Translator, *The Essential Rumi, New Expanded Edition*, (HarperOne, May 2004), 243.

2 Woodrow Wilson, "The Only Glory of America," *The Politics of Woodrow Wilson: Selections from His Speeches and Writings*, (Ayer Publishing, 1970), 239.

3 Eckhart Tolle, *A New Earth: Awakening to Your Life's Purpose*, (Penguin, January 2008), 258-269.

4 Paul Coelho, *The Alchemist*, (HarperCollins, Apr. 2006), 23.

5 Siddhartha Gautama, Quoted, Dalai Lama XIV, Author, *Mind of Clear Light: Advice on Living Well and Dying Consciously*, (Atria Books, Sep. 2004), 209.

6 Oscar Wilde, *Picture of Dorian Gray*, (Intervisual Books, Sep. 2011), 27.

7 Emma Goldman, *Anarchy and Other Essays*, (CreateSpace, Dec. 2009), 8.

8 Bob Marley, "Redemption Song," *Uprising*, 1980.

INCONCLUSIVE CONCLUSION…

1 *The Living Insights Study Bible, New International Version*, (The Zondervan Corporation, 1996), 1 John 4:7-8, 12.

2 Siddhartha Gautama, Quoted, Perry Garfinkel, Author, *Buddha or Bust: In Search of Truth, Meaning, Happiness, and the Man Who Found Them All*, (Three Rivers Press, Jul. 2007), 224.

3 *The Living Insights Study Bible, New International Version*, (The Zondervan Corporation, 1996), Job 34:3-4.

4 George Lucas, Director, *Star Wars: A New Hope*, "Obi-Wan," 1977.

5 Tony Bancroft, Director, Barry Cook, Director, *Walt Disney's Mulan*, "Emperor," 1998.

6 Terence McKenna, Quoted, Alex Burns, Author, *Terence McKenna: Mind Contagions*, old.disinfo.com/archive/pages/article/id1515/pg2 (Sep. 2001).

JOURNEY ON: INFLUENCES AND OTHER SOURCES

1 Isaac Newton, "Letter to Robert Hooke," (Feb. 15, 1676).

ABOUT THE AUTHOR

When the Skies Turn Red
Karen Neverland

When I was born, my eyes were connected directly to my heartbeat,
and each time it pulsed I pulled the whole Universe in.

That was until the first time I heard anger.

Hate split apart the Universe I held in each eye as I realized that what sprang
from nothing also must return there and fear was born within me.

But I rewrapped my essence into a gift paper covered presence
and I gave away myself in the most beautiful of methods.

By the time I found words I had already defined reality into what
people thought of me, with an ego to prove my complacency.

The Universe pulled back from my eyes because I was now defined
by the words I could speak and the things I could see.

Then school gave me a pencil to permanently prove my reality physically.

We memorized periodic tables and were periodically labeled as smart
for repeating ideas on command, rather than creating our own.

We were taught to forget our heartbeats in favor of the theories
behind them, because realness is only in what you read.

We were taught to sell our gold-encrusted eyes for the "good life" where we
traveled blind, walking along roads full of other expressionless eyes that confuse
our lies with True Beauty.

Evolution robbed us of our vision since we no longer used it;
now they told us all we needed to know.

In a classroom they told us:
"The skies are always blue."
"The skies are always blue."
"THE SKIES ARE ALWAYS BLUE."
"What kind of a fool are you to depict them differently?"
"What kind of a fool are you to act irrationally."
"Distract yourself with our numbers and facts."
"Magic is for the deluded."

Even as they polluted my seas, changed my sunsets from
orange to green, and replaced my grass with plastic.

A system of eight hours a day beat me down, until I was more lost than
found, feeling around in the dark for a life that lay inside of me.

My daytimes were spent dreaming, believing that the skies are always blue.

My dreams were replaced with television scenes; a sleep that
sewed my eye-sockets into sunken, star-struck fantasies.

The roses in my cheeks wilted, yielding only thorns in my eyes.

Smiles, once sweet as a chocolate-shop, locked together
into a rotten-caramel cemented grimace laced in venom.

My Kundalini snake snapped with poison jaws, until
my Garden of Eden became a decayed wasteland.

I stayed there for a really long time.

My saving grace is that I don't remember most of that self-serving hell.

You don't remember much when you're a shell, and
time passes quickly when you're not living at all.

But one day the Love-Force entered my Life Source.

AS WITHIN, SO WITHOUT

I suddenly saw the words: "Love Movement"
staring back at me from bathroom stalls.

Either one person was following me everywhere, or there was a
radical Revolution of Love happening from the bottom up.

I found myself scrawling the words "Live, Laugh, Love,"
on available blank walls, and "Love Matrix" in vacant halls.

I had awoken to a Heaven that was happening all
around me that I had been too blind to see.

And when it opened my eyes, my own Universe
was projected, rather than just reflected.

As I felt my heartbeat, for the first time in each moment,
I felt the Magic in Life, Love, and Laughing again.

And I dedicated my time to attaining all three, because you see,
textbooks don't teach the things worth living for.

And textbooks don't teach the things worth dying for.

So after 25 years of delays, here I am back at stage one,
but I'm having a lot more fun in this silly "System."

I'm ready to play without rules or restriction, by
breaking laws that are riddled in contradiction.

I'm ready for a few more pages in this Fiction;
I'm ready to be my own rhythm.

And you know, this time around…
I'm going to paint those skies red!

www.ingramcontent.com/pod-product-compliance
Lightning Source LLC
Chambersburg PA
CBHW071415160426
43195CB00013B/1704